CONTENTS

Piano/Vocal arrangements by Donald Sosin

Photography by Joan Marcus
Original show artwork courtesy of Serino Coyne, Inc.

ISBN 1-57560-616-X

Copyright © 2003 Cherry Lane Music Company
International Copyright Secured   All Rights Reserved

The music, text, design and graphics in this publication are protected by copyright law.
Any duplication or transmission, by any means, electronic, mechanical, photocopying,
recording or otherwise, is an infringement of copyright.

Visit our website at www.cherrylane.com

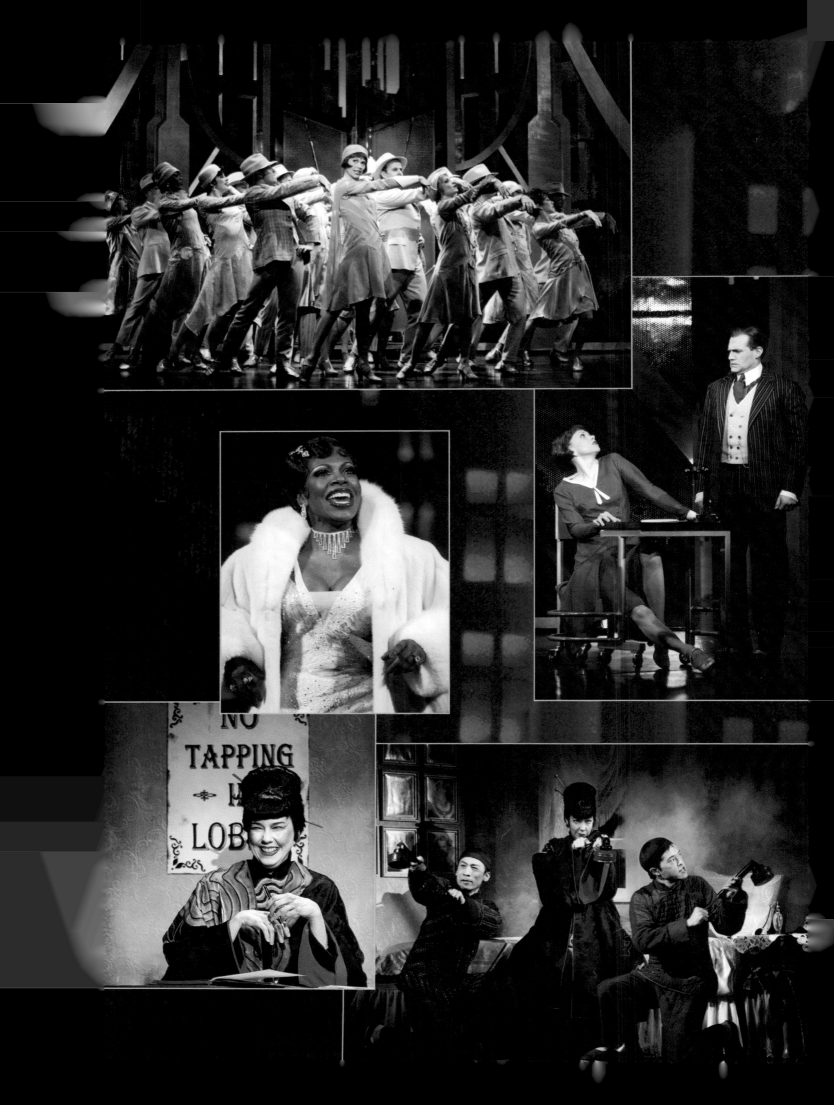

Michael Leavitt   Fox Theatricals   Hal Luftig
Stewart F. Lane   James L. Nederlander   Independent Presenters Network
L. Mages/M. Glick   Berinstein/Manocherian/Dramatic Forces   John York Noble
and Whoopi Goldberg

present

THOROUGHLY MODERN millie

THE NEW BROADWAY MUSICAL COMEDY

Book by **Richard Morris** and **Dick Scanlan**

New Music by **Jeanine Tesori**

New Lyrics by **Dick Scanlan**

Original Story and Screenplay by Richard Morris for the Universal Pictures Film

Starring

SHERYL LEE RALPH   HARRIET HARRIS   MARC KUDISCH
GAVIN CREEL   ANGELA CHRISTIAN
KEN LEUNG   FRANCIS JUE   ANNE L. NATHAN

With

Kate Baldwin   Roxane Barlow   Melissa Bell Chait   Catherine Brunell   Joyce Chittick   J.P. Christensen
Julie Connors   David Eggers   Aldrin Gonzalez   Gregg Goodbrod   Jessica Grové   Susan Haefner
Amy Heggins   JoAnn M. Hunter   Alisa Klein   Matt Lashey   Darren Lee   Dan LoBuono
Casey Nicholaw   Noah Racey   Aaron Ramey   T. Oliver Reid   Megan Sikora   Brandon Wardell

and introducing

SUTTON FOSTER
as Millie

Scenic Design	Costume Design	Lighting Design	Sound Design
DAVID GALLO	**MARTIN PAKLEDINAZ**	**DONALD HOLDER**	**JON WESTON**

Orchestrations	Dance Music Arranger	Vocal Music Arranger	Music Coordinator
DOUG BESTERMAN and **RALPH BURNS**	**DAVID CHASE**	**JEANINE TESORI**	**JOHN MILLER**

Hair Designer	Press Representative	Marketing	Casting
PAUL HUNTLEY	**BARLOW • HARTMAN**	**TMG—THE MARKETING GROUP**	**JIM CARNAHAN, C.S.A.**

Production Manager	General Management	Production Stage Manager	Associate Producers
THEATERSMITH, INC.	**NINA LANNAN ASSOCIATES**	**BONNIE L. BECKER**	**MIKE ISAACSON KRISTIN CASKEY**
			CLEAR CHANNEL ENTERTAINMENT

Music Director

MICHAEL RAFTER

Choreographed by

ROB ASHFORD

Directed by

MICHAEL MAYER

Originally Produced by La Jolla Playhouse, La Jolla, CA
Des McAnuff, Artistic Director & Terrence Dwyer, Managing Director

THE STORY

Manhattan. 1922. Millie Dillmount steps off the train from Salina, Kansas. She's read books and studied photos in preparation for her new life. The first step? A new look: bobbed hair and a short skirt turn Millie into a modern.

Her delight is short-lived when her purse is stolen. Millie calls out for help, but the hustling, bustling New Yorkers pay no attention, so she trips one of them. He's plenty mad at Millie, taking just enough pity on her to give her the address of a residence for young ladies. He also gives her advice: go back to Kansas, because she's clearly not Manhattan material. Determined to prove him wrong, she storms off to find the Hotel Priscilla.

A week later, she hasn't found a job. The girls at the Priscilla are worried because young girls are disappearing all over town. Mrs. Meers, the manager of the hotel, sets their minds at ease: unlike the Priscilla girls, the kidnapping victims are orphans. Relieved, the girls head out on auditions. Only Ethel Peas remains, clutching a telegram informing her of the death of her only remaining relative, leaving Ethel an orphan. Bad news for Ethel, but good news for Mrs. Meers, whose real name is Daisy Crumpler. The Priscilla is a front for her real occupation: kidnapping orphan girls and shipping them into slavery. Two young Chinese immigrants, Ching Ho and Bun Foo, reluctantly act as her henchmen because of her promise to bring their mother to America.

While Mrs. Meers is in her office doping Ethel Peas, Millie returns to the Priscilla, still unemployed. Miss Dorothy Brown, a wealthy orphan, checks in. She and Millie strike up an immediate friendship. Dorothy reveals her dream to be an actress, and Millie reveals her dream to parlay her typing skills into a job for an eligible bachelor, and then marry him.

Later that day, Millie finds her dream boss, a successful bachelor named Trevor Graydon III. Despite Millie's attempts to flirt with him, Trevor is interested only in her secretarial skills, which land Millie the job.

Back at the Priscilla, Mrs. Meers lays a trap for Dorothy. She sends a drugged apple to Dorothy's room, with Ching Ho playing waiter. The moment he lays eyes on Dorothy, Ching Ho can't go through with it. He's immediately smitten, so Mrs. Meers takes over. However, her attempts to convince Dorothy to eat the apple are interrupted by girls coming and going.

Millie takes Dorothy and the girls out that night to celebrate her new job. This is the height of Prohibition, when selling alcohol was illegal, and the girls don't know how to find a speakeasy. Help comes from an unlikely source: the man who Millie tripped after she was mugged. His name is Jimmy Smith, and though he and Millie are cool to each other, he's impressed by her new confidence. He sneaks them into a nearby speakeasy, where they have their first taste of booze and dance the night away. As the evening progresses, so do Jimmy's feelings for Millie, and the two of them are finding it difficult to resist their growing attraction. The fun comes to a halt when police raid the joint, landing Jimmy and Millie in prison overnight. While everyone sleeps in their cells, Jimmy realizes that he is falling in love with Millie.

The next morning, Jimmy asks Millie out. When she tells him about Trevor, Jimmy is crestfallen. To save face, he insists that his interest in Millie is platonic, and he proves his point by asking her to bring Dorothy along.

For the next few weeks, Millie, Dorothy and Jimmy are inseparable. Jimmy is their guide to New York nightlife, but the topper comes when he wrangles an invitation to a party at the penthouse of a world-famous singer named Muzzy Van Hossmere. The cream of New York society is there, but Jimmy only has eyes for Millie. Alone on Muzzy's terrace, they argue about her plan to marry her boss, and in the midst of their angry words, they kiss. And what a kiss, enough to make Millie realize that she's falling in love with him, too. She returns to the Priscilla on a cloud of love, but she's brought back to earth when, to her astonishment, she sees Jimmy sneaking out of Dorothy's bedroom.

The next day, at work, Millie slams the phone down whenever Jimmy calls her. She is further aggravated by Dorothy, who drops by after a bad audition. Millie's day goes from bad to worse when Trevor is immediately captivated by Dorothy's beauty. Trevor asks Dorothy to dinner, and she accepts; in a few short minutes, Millie has lost her boss/fiancé and her best friend.

Jimmy then appears at the window. Lovestruck, he has climbed up 20 stories to the ledge outside Millie's window, and refuses to leave until she speaks to him. Millie confronts him about his visit to Dorothy's room, and Jimmy explains that he went there for some advice regarding his love for Millie. Millie can't help but give in to her feelings: they agree to meet that night for dinner at Café Society, where Muzzy will be singing.

That night, Millie and Jimmy come up short for Café Society's pricey bill. They're banished to the kitchen, washing dishes to pay for their dinner. Millie is elbow deep in soapsuds when she realizes that life with Jimmy will mean a life she'd hoped to escape by leaving Kansas. She may love him, but to Millie, modern marriage means money. She bolts from the kitchen and into Muzzy's dressing room. Muzzy convinces Millie that, when it comes to marriage, love is all that matters.

Millie is determined to find Jimmy and make up with him, but she is stopped by a drunken Trevor. Millie is stunned to learn that when Trevor went to the Hotel Priscilla to pick Dorothy up for their date, Mrs. Meers told him that Dorothy had checked out. Jimmy enters, and his joy at finding Millie is overshadowed by his concern for the disappeared Dorothy. It doesn't take them long to figure out that Mrs. Meers has kidnapped Dorothy and plans to sell her into slavery. Millie devises a plan to save the day.

Muzzy checks into the Priscilla disguised as a new orphan in town. Mrs. Meers sees through Muzzy's act, so Muzzy goads Mrs. Meers into bragging about her criminal endeavors. Millie, Trevor, and Jimmy emerge from their hiding places, where Millie has taken down every word of Mrs. Meers' confession in shorthand. Who ends up with whom? A series of surprise revelations guarantees a thoroughly happy ending for all!

JEANINE TESORI (Composer)

Jeanine Tesori is an award-winning composer for theatre, film, television, and recordings. Along with librettist/lyricist Dick Scanlan, Ms. Tesori wrote the score for *Thoroughly Modern Millie*, which won the 2002 Tony and Drama Desk Awards for Best Musical, and earned her Tony, Drama Desk, and Grammy nominations. She also scored Nicholas Hytner's production of *Twelfth Night* at Lincoln Center Theater, for which she received a 1999 Drama Desk Award and her first Tony nomination. With librettist/lyricist Brian Crawley, Ms. Tesori wrote the widely acclaimed musical *Violet*, which was produced at Playwrights Horizons. *Violet* was named Best Musical by the NY Drama Critics Circle and the Lucille Lortel Awards, and Ms. Tesori received an Obie Award for her music. For film, in collaboration with lyricist Alexa Junge, Ms. Tesori has written the score for *Mulan II* and contributed songs to *Lilo and Stitch II*, both due out from Disney next year. Ms. Tesori was commissioned by Sony Classical to write the song "The Girl in 14G" (with words by Dick Scanlan) for Kristin Chenoweth's debut CD, *Let Yourself Go*. Ms. Tesori and Mr. Scanlan also wrote the theme song to Ms. Chenoweth's NBC/Paramount sitcom, *Kristin*. As for future projects, Ms. Tesori is currently writing *Caroline, or Change*, with libretto and lyrics by Tony Kushner, which will receive its world premiere at the Public Theatre in Fall 2003 under the direction of George C. Wolfe. Ms. Tesori began her Broadway career as conductor and arranger of such shows as *Tommy, Big River*, and *The Secret Garden*. While playing piano in the pit for the Tyne Daly revival of *Gypsy*, she fell in love with its music director, Michael Rafter. They are now the proud parents of five-year-old Siena, named after the Italian town in which they were married.

DICK SCANLAN (Lyricist)

Dick Scanlan wrote the book and lyrics for 2002's Tony and Drama Desk Award Winning Best Musical, *Thoroughly Modern Millie*, a stage adaptation of the 1967 Universal film. For *Thoroughly Modern Millie*, his first Broadway outing, Mr. Scanlan was nominated for two Tony Awards (Best Book and Best Score), two Drama Desk Awards, and a Grammy Award. Along with Jeanine Tesori, *Thoroughly Modern Millie's* composer, Mr. Scanlan was commissioned to compose a song for Broadway sensation Kristin Chenoweth in connection with *Let Yourself Go*, her debut album on Sony. That song, "The Girl in 14G," has been performed at Lincoln Center and in concert halls across America as well as having been a critics' favorite during Ms. Chenoweth's sold-out run at London's Donmar Warehouse. Mr. Scanlan and Ms. Tesori also wrote the theme song to Ms. Chenoweth's NBC/Paramount sitcom, *Kristin*. In addition to his work for the theatre, Mr. Scanlan is a noted fiction writer. His novel, *Does Freddy Dance*, was published in 1995 to glowing reviews and was reissued in paperback in 1997, both by Alyson Publications. His short fiction has been seen in numerous literary and commercial magazines, and is included in *Best American Gay Fiction 1996* (Little, Brown) along with such luminaries as Edmund White and Michael Cunningham. His essays and articles on the arts have appeared in the "Arts & Leisure" section of *The New York Times, The New Yorker, Vanity Fair, The Village Voice, Playboy, Time Out New York, Men's Style, TheaterWeek, Show People, Genre*, and other magazines. Mr. Scanlan has served as the theatre critic for *The Advocate* and as acting editor-in-chief for *POZ*, an award-winning national magazine for people living with HIV. A former actor, Mr. Scanlan originated the role of Miss Great Plains in the hit Off-Broadway musical *Pageant*.

2002 TONY AWARDS®

Best Choreography—Rob Ashford
Best Orchestrations—Doug Besterman & Ralph Burns
Best Costume Design—Martin Pakledinaz
Best Performance by a Featured Actress in a Musical—Harriet Harris
Best Performance by a Leading Actress in a Musical—Sutton Foster
Best Musical—Thoroughly Modern Millie

Not for the Life of Me

Lyrics by Dick Scanlan

Music by Jeanine Tesori

Copyright © 2001 That's Music To My Ears Ltd. and Thoroughly Modern Music Publishing Co.
International Copyright Secured   All Rights Reserved

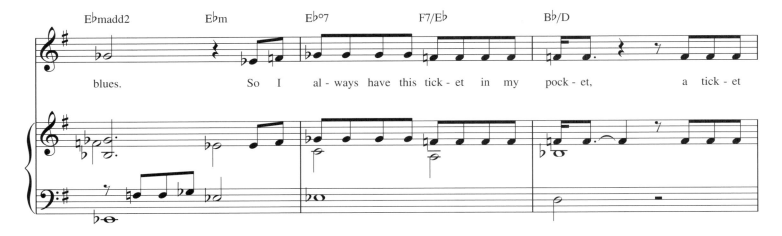

blues.   So   I   al - ways   have   this   tick - et   in   my   pock - et,   a   tick - et

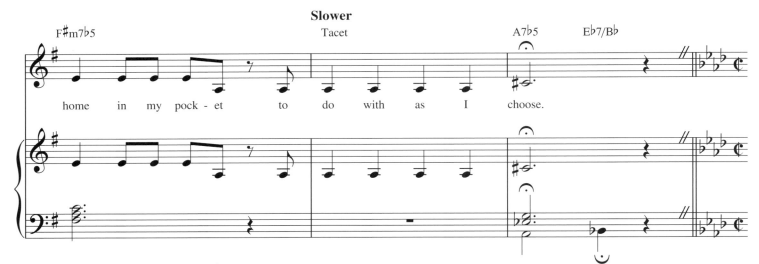

home   in   my   pock - et   to   do   with   as   I   choose.

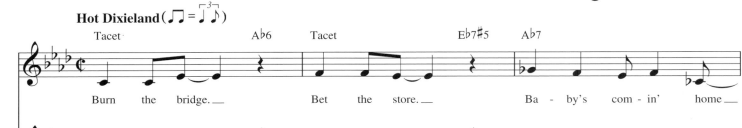

Burn   the   bridge. ___   Bet   the   store. ___   Ba - by's   com - in'   home ___

___   no   more. ___   Not   for   the   life   of   me.

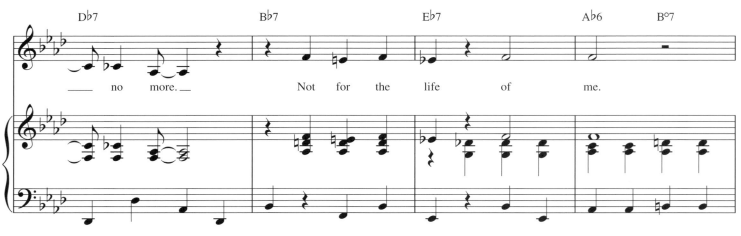

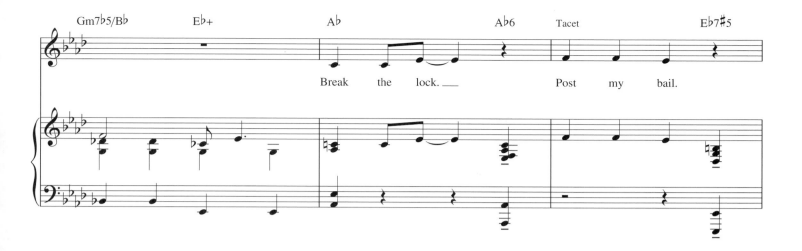

Break the lock. ___ Post my bail.

Done my time, I'm out-ta jail. ___ Not for the

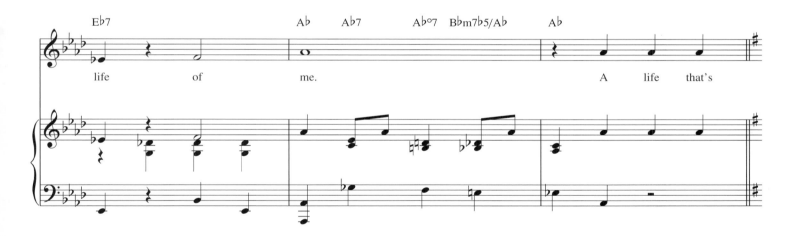

life of me. A life that's

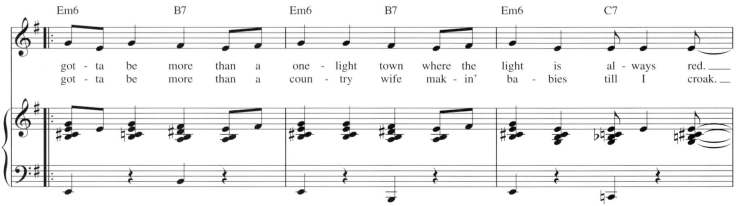

got-ta be more than a one-light town where the light is al-ways red. ___
got-ta be more than a coun-try wife mak-in' ba-bies till I croak. ___

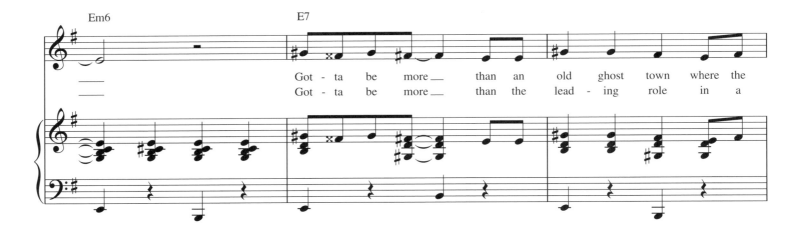

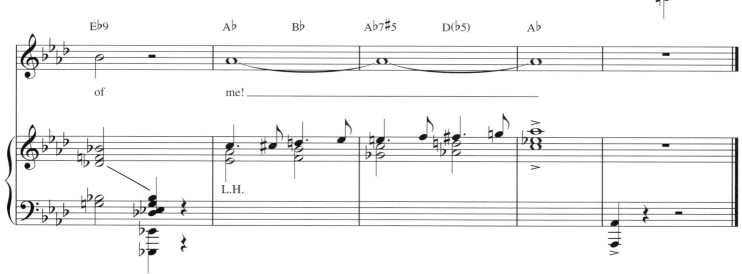

Thoroughly Modern Millie

Words by Sammy Cahn

Music by James Van Heusen

Copyright © 1967; Renewed 1995 Cahn Music Company (ASCAP) and Universal - Northern Music Company, Inc. (ASCAP)
All Rights for Cahn Music Company Administered by Cherry Lane Music Publishing Company, Inc. and DreamWorks Songs
International Copyright Secured   All Rights Reserved

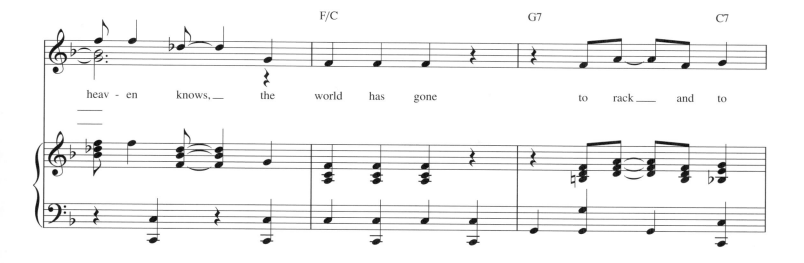

heav-en knows, ___ the world has gone to rack ___ and to

ruin.

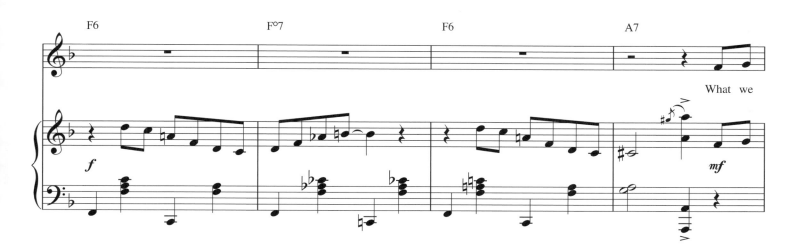

What we

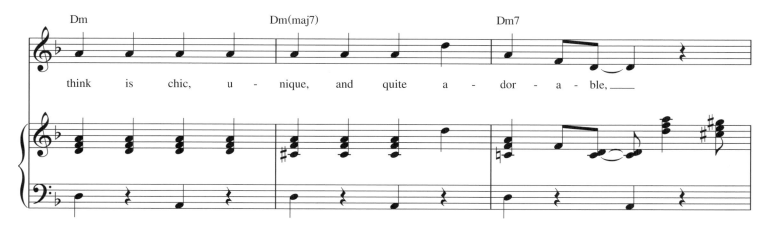

think is chic, u - nique, and quite a - dor - a - ble, ___

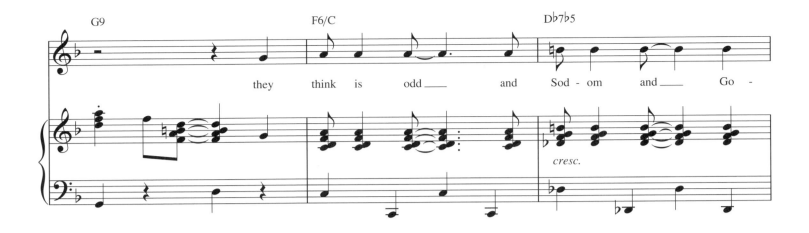

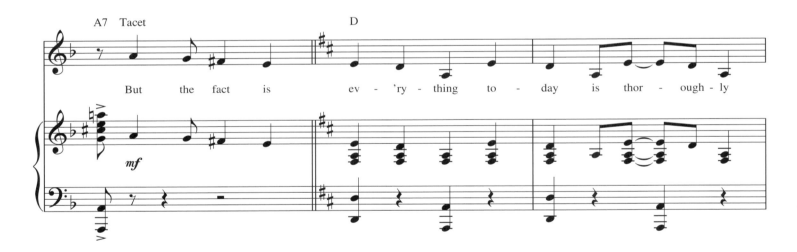

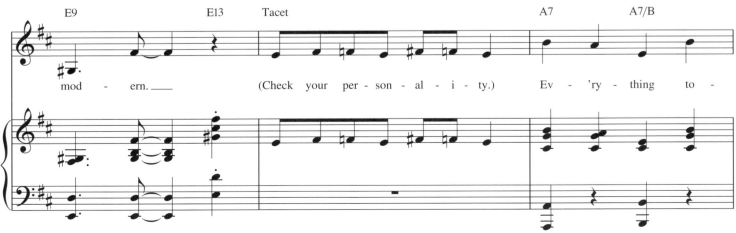

day makes yes - ter - day slow. (Bet - ter face re - al - i - ty.)

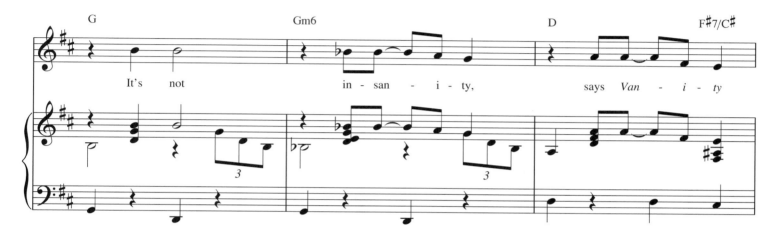

It's not in - san - i - ty, says *Van - i - ty*

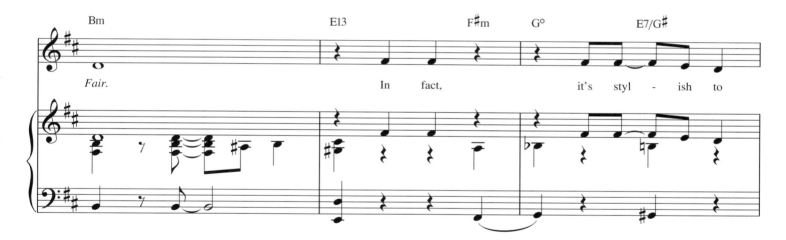

Fair. In fact, it's styl - ish to

raise your skirts and bob your hair, _____
Raise your skirts and bob your hair, _____
Raise your skirts and

bob your hair! ___
bob your hair! ___
Have you seen the way they kiss ___ in the

mov - ies? ___ (Is - n't it de - lect - a - ble?) Paint - ing lips and

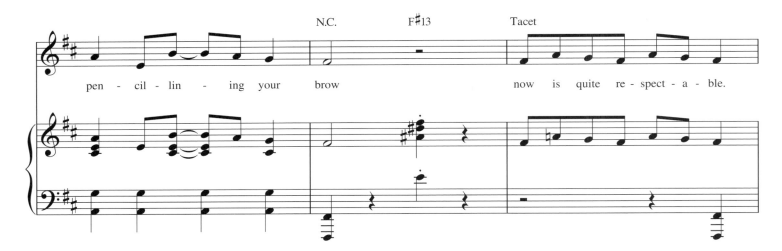

pen - cil - lin - ing your brow now is quite re - spect - a - ble.

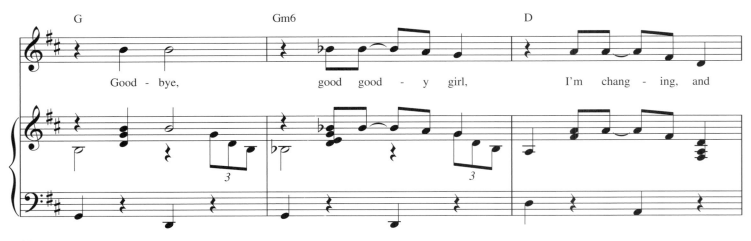

Good - bye, good good - y girl, I'm chang - ing, and

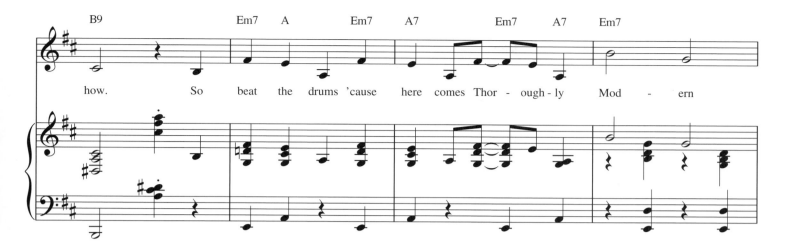

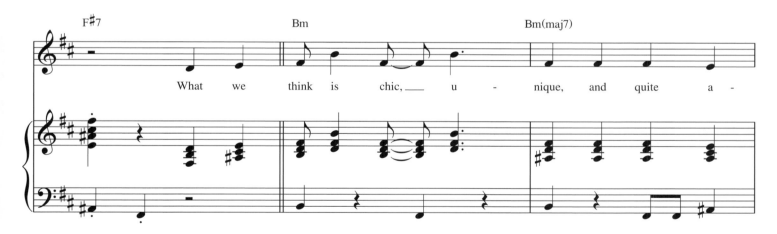

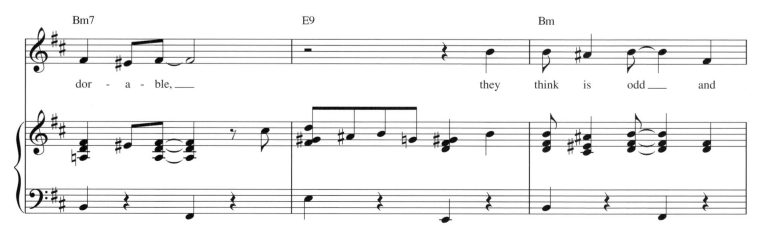

Sod - om and ___ Go - mor - rah - ble! ___ But the fact is,

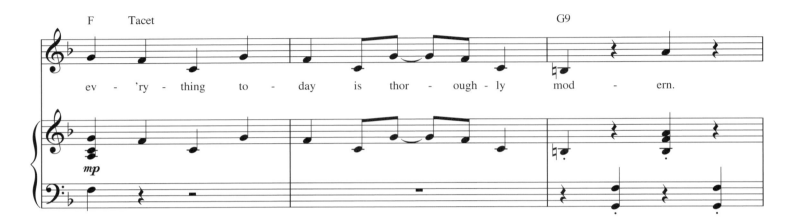

ev - 'ry - thing to - day is thor - ough - ly mod - ern.

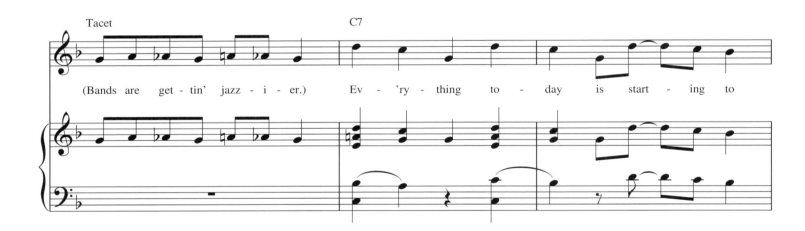

(Bands are get - tin' jazz - i - er.) Ev - 'ry - thing to - day is start - ing to

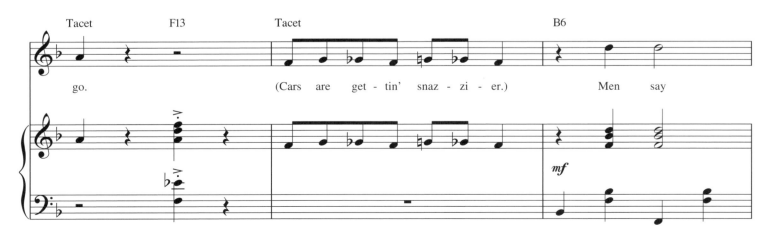

go. (Cars are get - tin' snaz - zi - er.) Men say

it's crim - i - nal   what wom - en - 'll   do.

What they're   for - get - ting is   this   is   nine - teen

twen - ty - two! ___

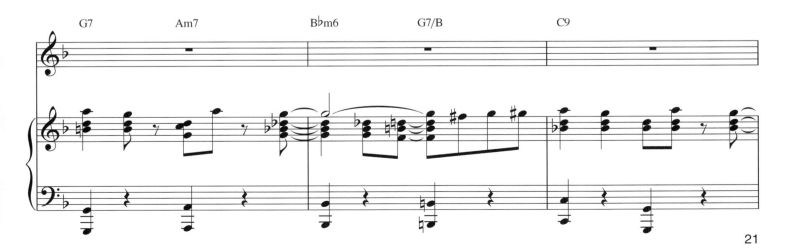

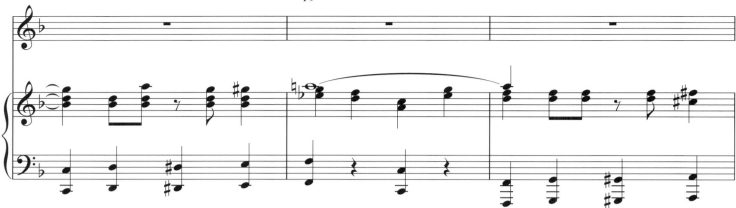

Good - bye, good good -

y girl, I'm chang - ing, and how!

I'm chang - ing, and how! So

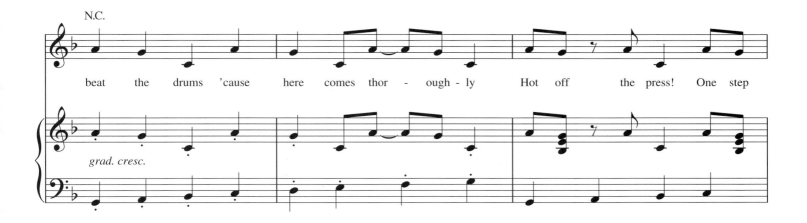

beat the drums 'cause here comes thor - ough - ly Hot off the press! One step

a - head! Jazz Age! Whoop - ee, ba - by! We're so Thor - ough - ly

Gm7   Tacet

Mod - ern _____ Mil - lie

F   D♭7   F6

now! _____

How the Other Half Lives

Lyrics by Dick Scanlan

Music by Jeanine Tesori

Copyright © 2001 That's Music To My Ears Ltd. and Thoroughly Modern Music Publishing Co.
International Copyright Secured   All Rights Reserved

Let me brown bag all my lunch - es, try my hand at canned

cui - sine. A Ber - litz class I long to pass.

How the oth - er half, how the oth - er half lives! No four - teen car - at

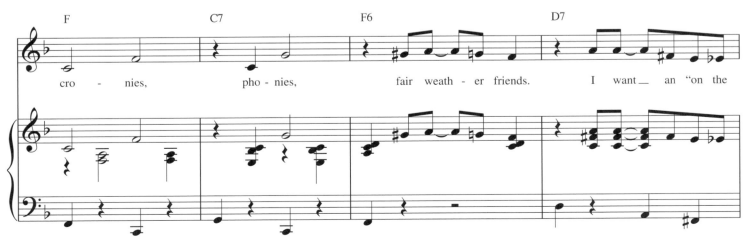

cro - nies, pho - nies, fair weath - er friends. I want an "on the

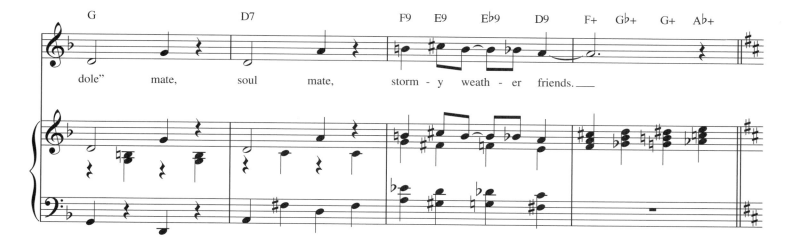

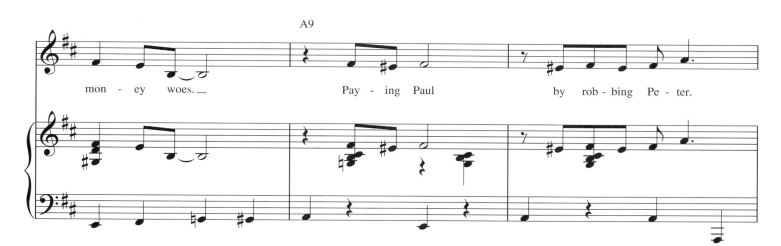

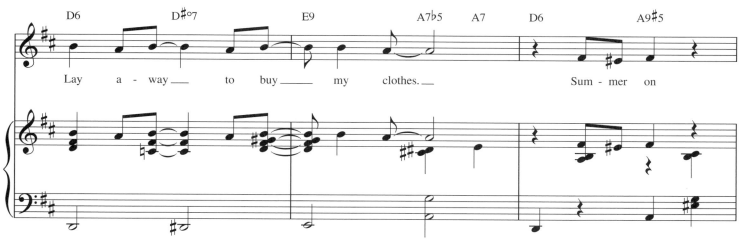

the isle of Con - ey. Win - ter in ____ Hell's kitch - en - ette. ____ I'll

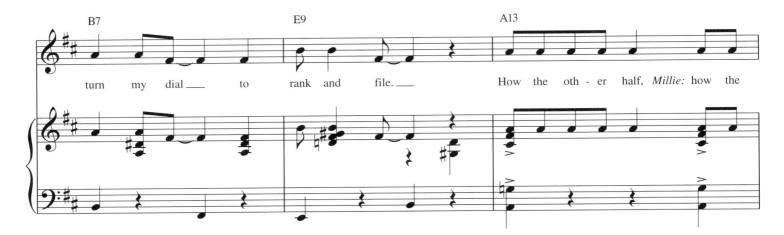

turn my dial ____ to rank and file. ____ How the oth - er half, *Millie:* how the

oth - er half lives! Poor? Not me, hon - ey. I don't want those

mon - ey woes. I'll mar - ry Paul or Dave or Rob or Pe - ter

so I can buy my clothes at Saks Fifth Av-e-nue,

Berg - dorf Good - man, too! The priv - 'leged few plus

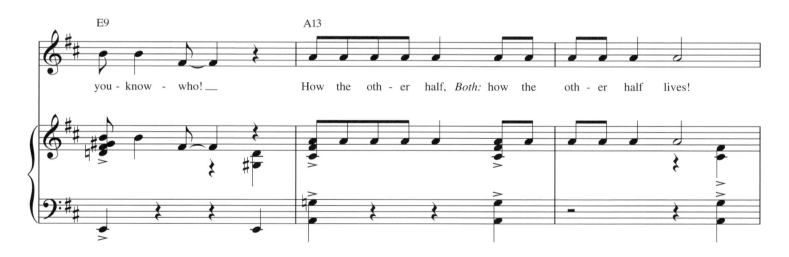

you - know - who! How the oth - er half, *Both:* how the oth - er half lives!

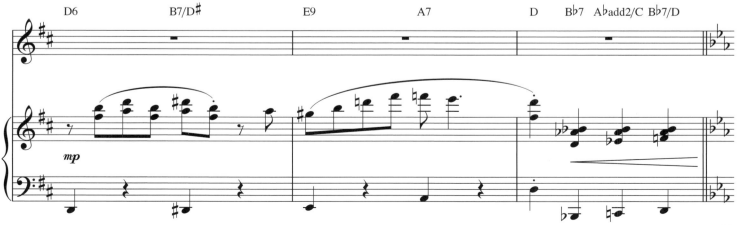

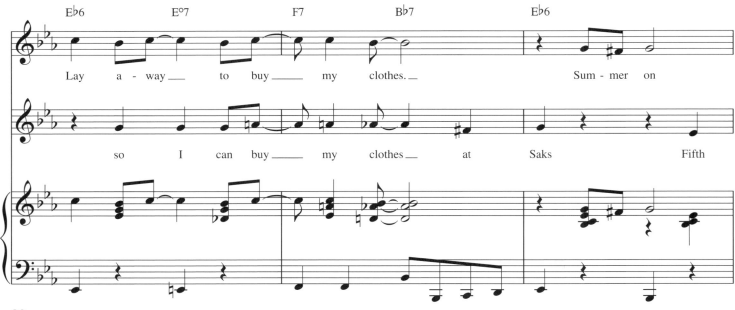

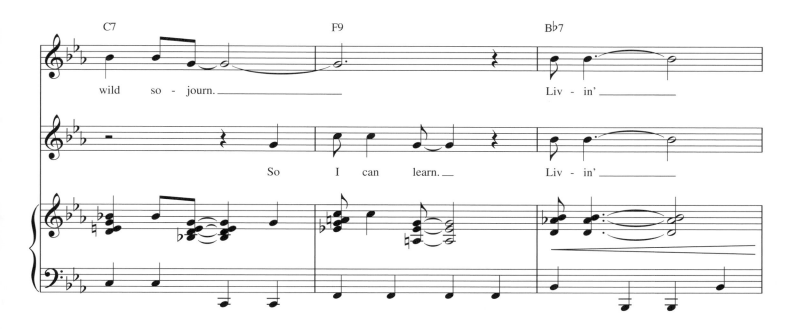

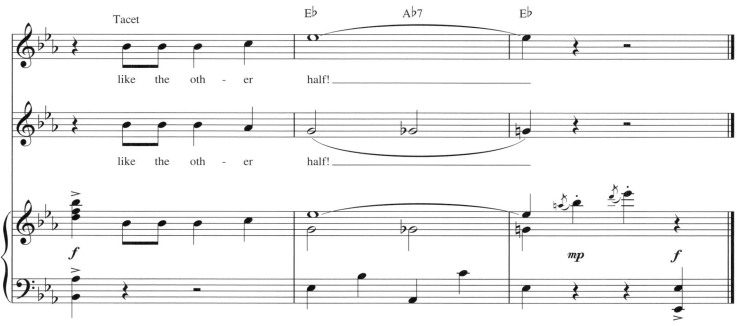

31

The Speed Test

Lyrics by Dick Scanlan

Music by Arthur Sullivan

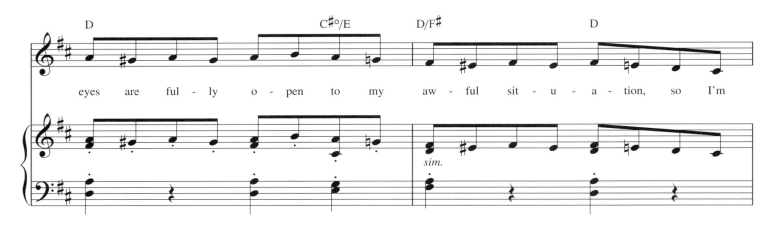

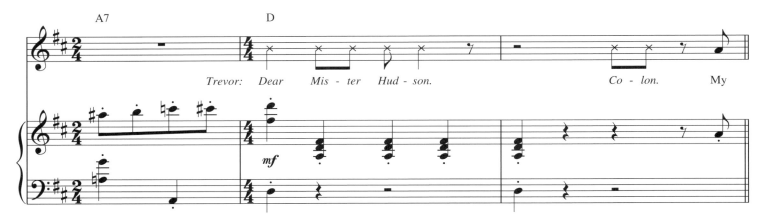

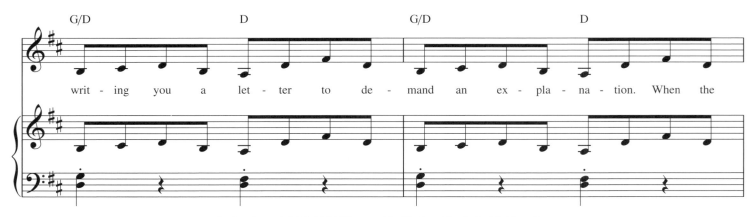

Lyrics Copyright © 2001 Thoroughly Modern Music Publishing Co.
This Arrangement Copyright © 2001 That's Music To My Ears Ltd.
International Copyright Secured   All Rights Reserved

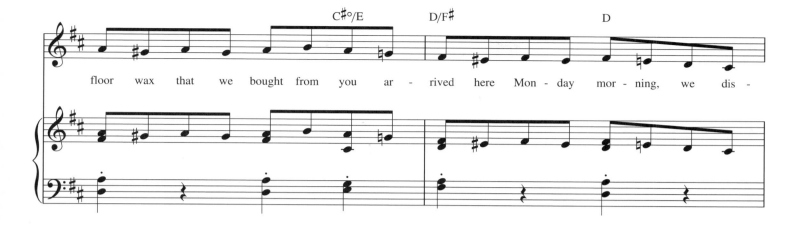

floor wax that we bought from you ar - rived here Mon - day mor - ning, we dis -

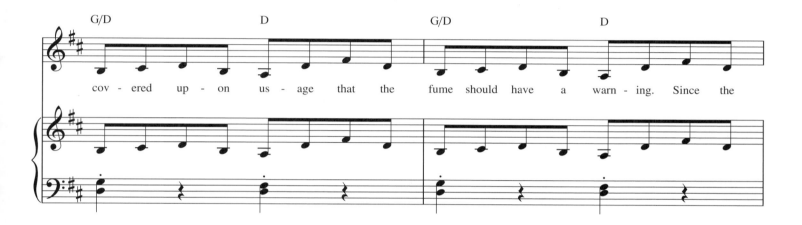

cov - ered up - on us - age that the fume should have a warn - ing. Since the

on - ly pos - si - bil - i - ty is that your wax is ran - cid, I re -

quest a full re - fund of all the mon - ey we ad - van - ced. And un -

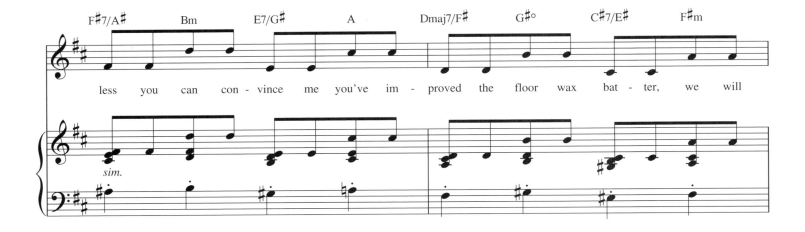

F#7/A# Bm E7/G# A Dmaj7/F# G#° C#7/E# F#m

less you can con - vince me you've im - proved the floor wax bat - ter, we will

sim.

D6 Bm7 E7 A

take our bus' - ness else - where, so I hope you solve this mat - ter.

A little faster

D

(Spoken:) How's my speed, Miss Dillmount?   *Millie: A little slow, perhaps.*   *Trevor:* En -

mf

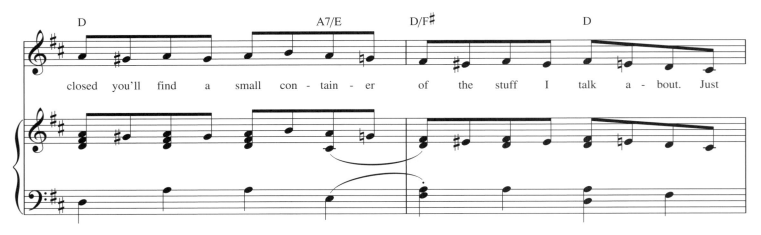

D A7/E D/F# D

closed you'll find a small con - tain - er of the stuff I talk a - bout. Just

34

care - ful - ly re - move the lid and take a whiff if you've a doubt. I'm

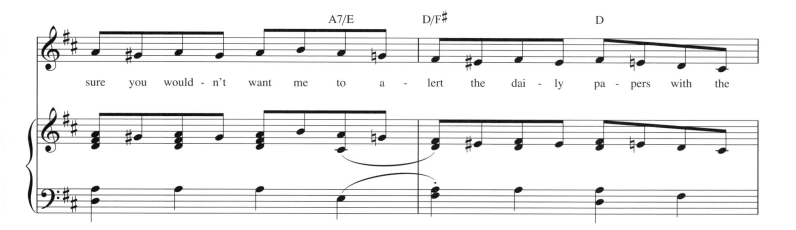

sure you would-n't want me to a - lert the dai - ly pa - pers with the

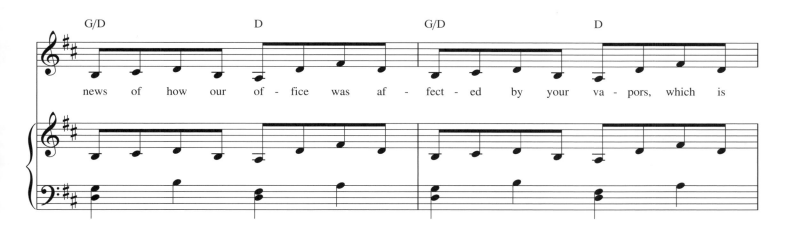

news of how our of - fice was af - fect - ed by your va - pors, which is

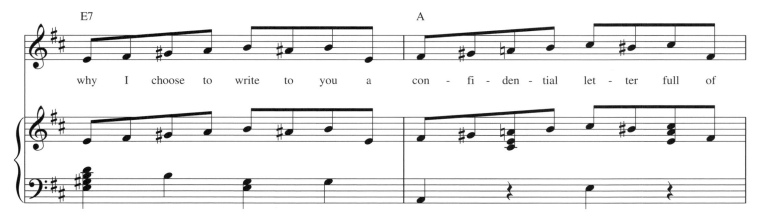

why I choose to write to you a con - fi - den - tial let - ter full of

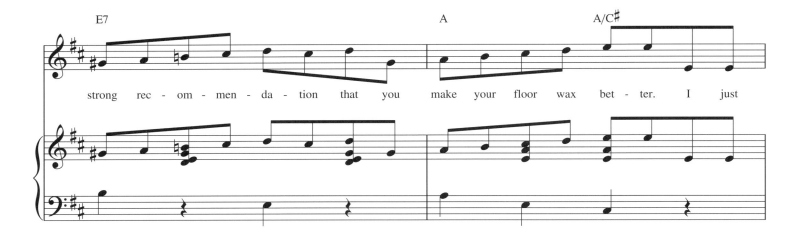

strong rec - om - men - da - tion that you make your floor wax bet - ter. I just

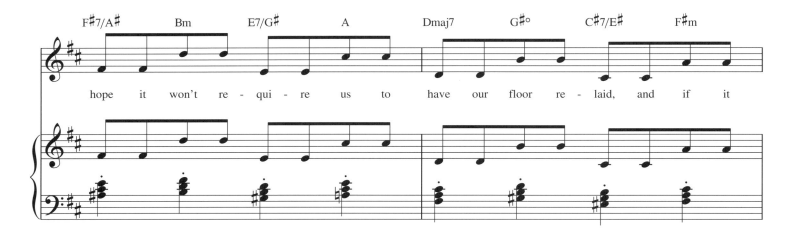

hope it won't re - qui - re us to have our floor re - laid, and if it

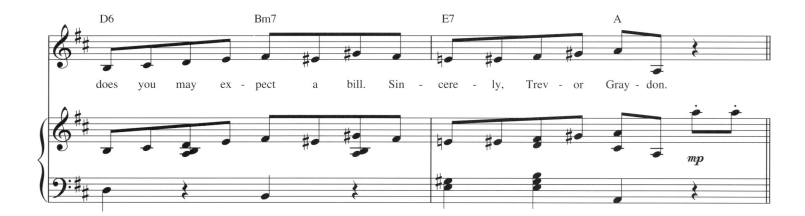

does you may ex - pect a bill. Sin - cere - ly, Trev - or Gray - don.

A little faster

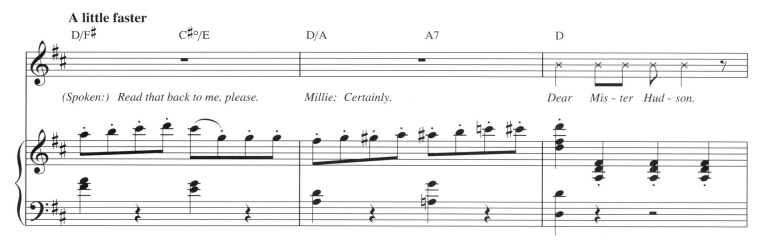

(Spoken:) Read that back to me, please.   Millie: Certainly.   Dear Mis - ter Hud - son.

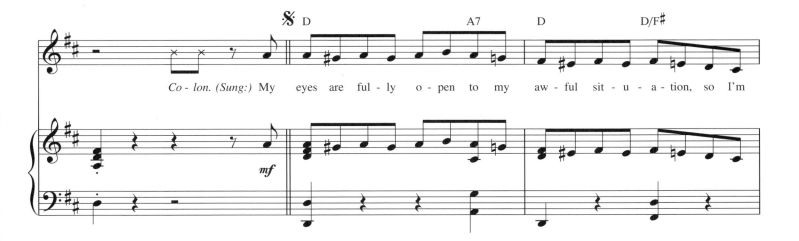

Co - lon. (Sung:) My eyes are ful - ly o - pen to my aw - ful sit - u - a - tion, so I'm

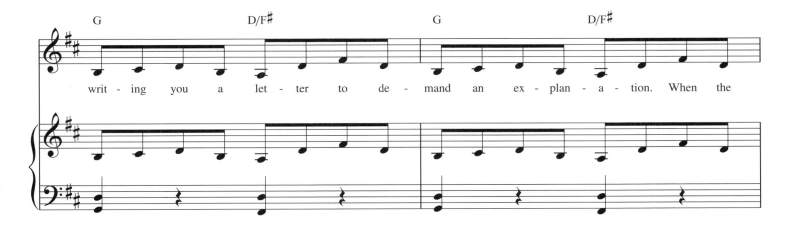

writ - ing you a let - ter to de - mand an ex - plan - a - tion. When the

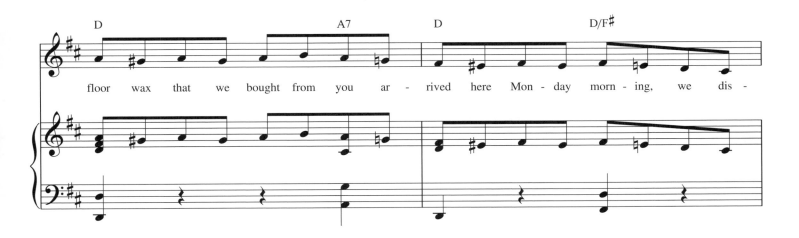

floor wax that we bought from you ar - rived here Mon - day morn - ing, we dis -

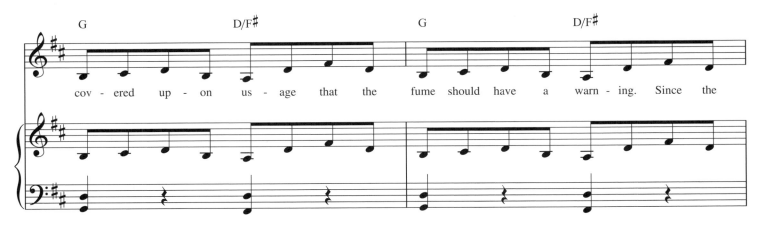

cov - ered up - on us - age that the fume should have a warn - ing. Since the

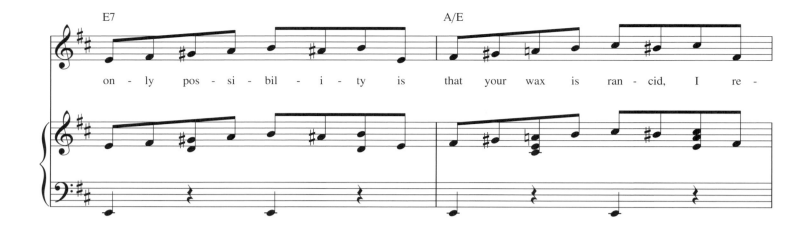

on - ly pos - si - bil - i - ty is that your wax is ran - cid, I re -

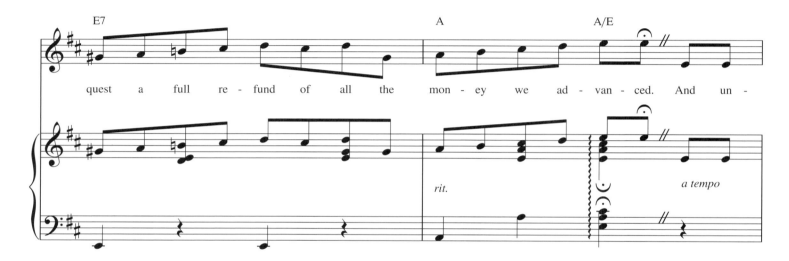

quest a full re - fund of all the mon - ey we ad - van - ced. And un -

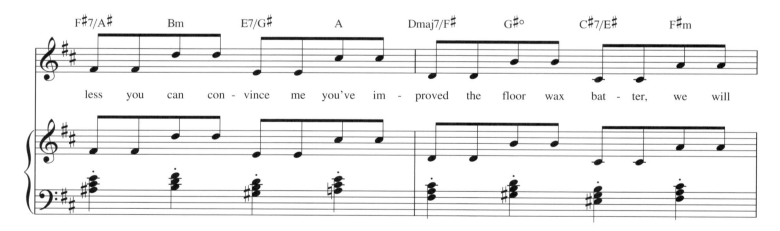

less you can con - vince me you've im - proved the floor wax bat - ter, we will

take our bus' - ness else - where, so I hope you solve this mat - ter.

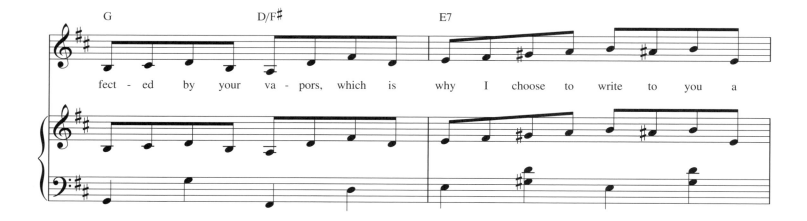

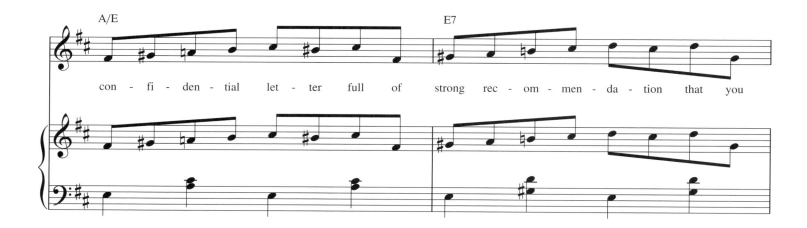

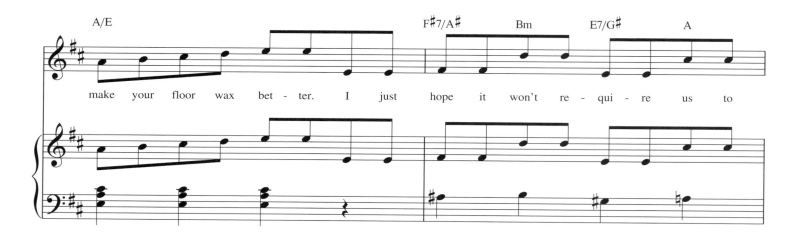

cere - ly, Trev - or Gray - don. *Trevor: Miss Dillmount, may I speak frankly?* *Millie: Yes?* *Trevor: If*

Moderately slow, freely

I could be so luck - y as to have a good sten - og - raph - er to

keep this place as up to date as her short skirt and bobbed coif - fure, I

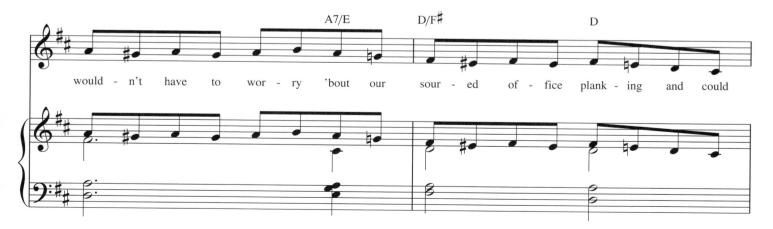

would - n't have to wor - ry 'bout our sour - ed of - fice plank - ing and could

con- cen- trate on gen- er- at- ing prof- its ripe for bank- ing. That is

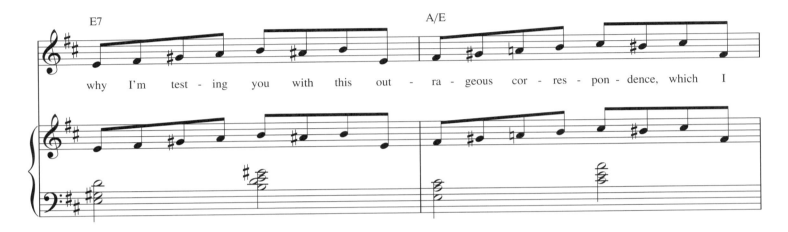

why I'm test- ing you with this out- ra- geous cor- res- pon- dence, which I

don't in- tend to ac- tu- al- ly mail to the re- spon- dents. So if

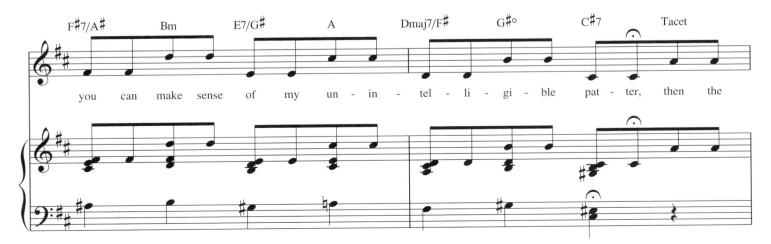

you can make sense of my un- in- tel- li- gi- ble pat- ter, then the

Briskly

job is yours and Hud - son's floor wax real - ly does - n't mat - ter. Hud - son's

Trevor: floor wax does - n't mat - ter? Hud - son's *Millie:* floor wax does - n't mat - ter. Hud - son's

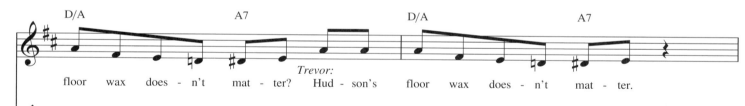

Trevor: floor wax does - n't mat - ter? Hud - son's floor wax does - n't mat - ter.

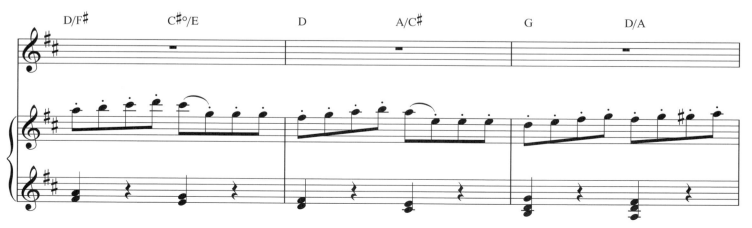

Trevor: Dear Mis - ter Hud - son.   *All:* Co - lon. *Trevor:* My

*From this point, recorded a half step higher than written.

Coda

Moderately slow

cere - ly, Trev - or Gray - don. You have made the team, Miss Dill - mount! You have

Chorus:

made the team, Miss Dill - mount! Tell me where my desk is, when we eat lunch,

Millie:

how much I'll be paid, and nice to meet you, I know we'll be friends, just

grad. accel.

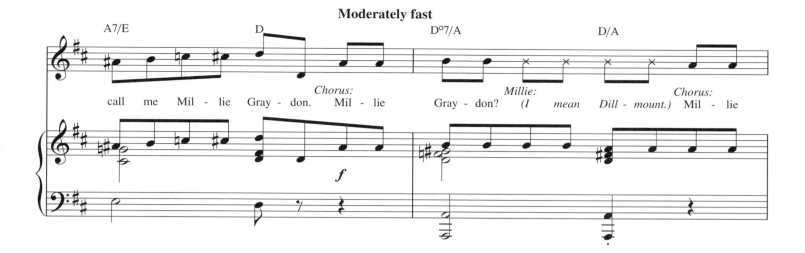

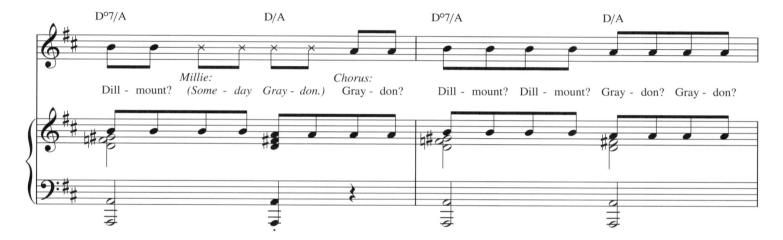

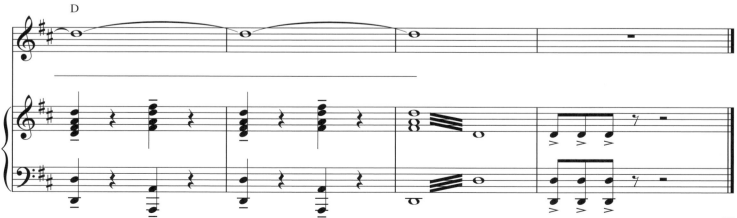

They Don't Know

Lyrics by Dick Scanlan

Music by Jeanine Tesori

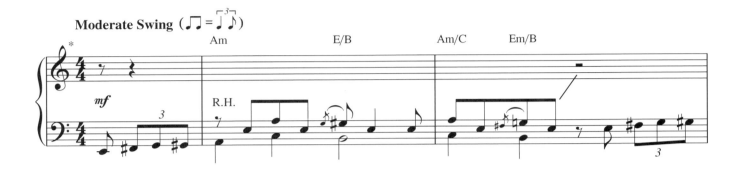

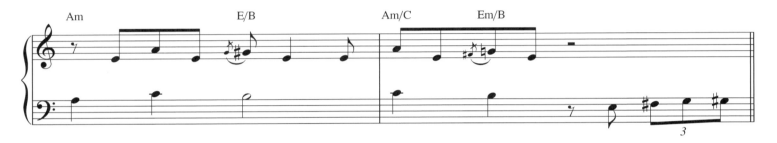

*Recorded a half step lower.

Copyright © 2001 That's Music To My Ears Ltd. and Thoroughly Modern Music Publishing Co.
International Copyright Secured   All Rights Reserved

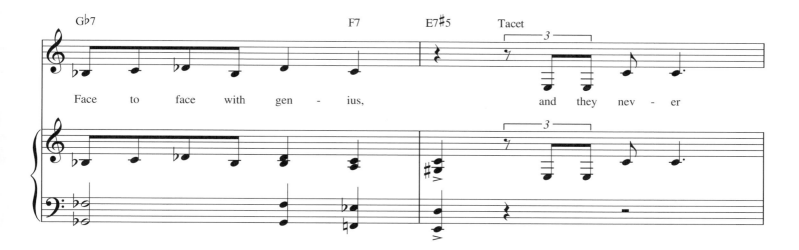

Face to face with gen - ius, and they nev - er

guess.

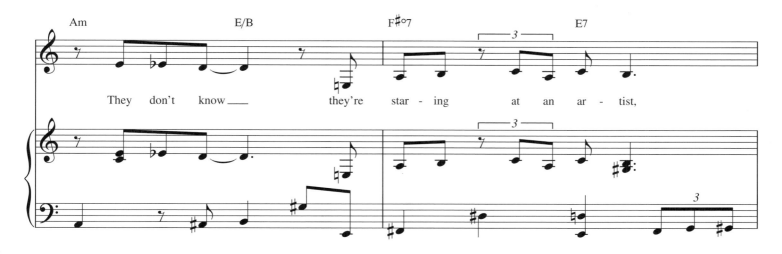

They don't know ___ they're star - ing at an ar - tist,

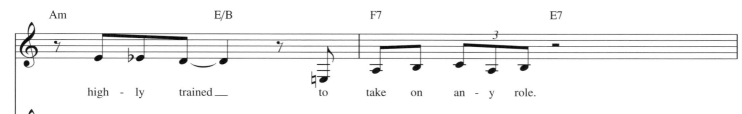

high - ly trained ___ to take on an - y role.

Skill - ful mime and bril - liant laun - dry cart - ist,

seek - ing ret - ri - bu - tion for the life they stole. I

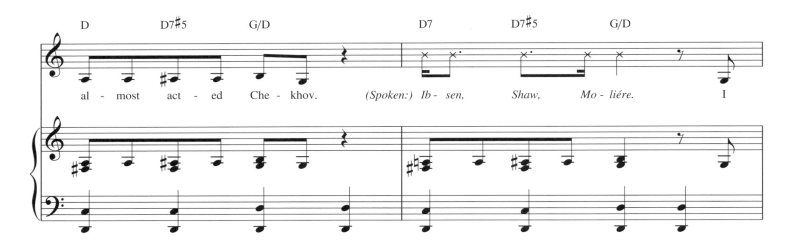

al - most act - ed Che - khov. *(Spoken:) Ib - sen, Shaw, Mo - liére.* I

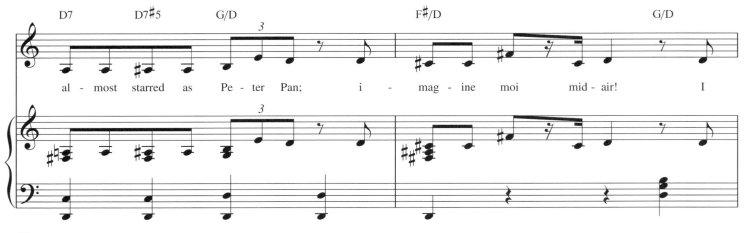

al - most starred as Pe - ter Pan; i - mag - ine moi mid - air! I

No Swing (♪♪ = ♪♪)

al - most tack - led Shake - speare, a blush - ing Ju - li - et. And

Swing (♪♪ = ♪³♪)

if the house were big e - nough, I still could play her yet!

They don't know ___ I'm hot - ter news ___ than Du - se,

Hel - en Hayes, ___ and Bern - hardt all in one. ___

They're on top _____ and I look like a los - uh.

Wait and see who's stand - ing when my play is

done. So wel - come, all ye bright young la - dies,

you're check - ing in - to Ho - tel Ha - des. I won't stand by while

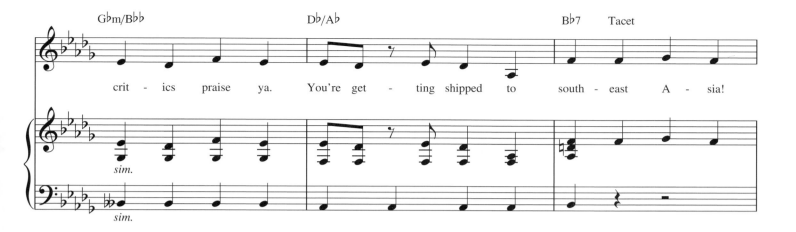

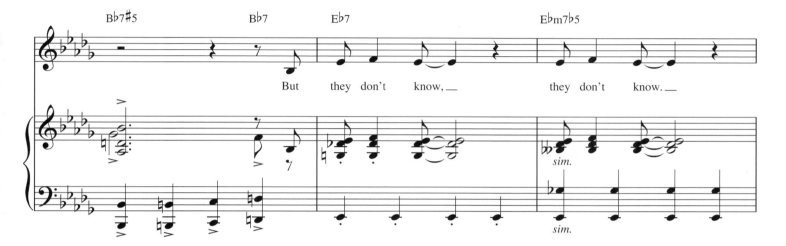

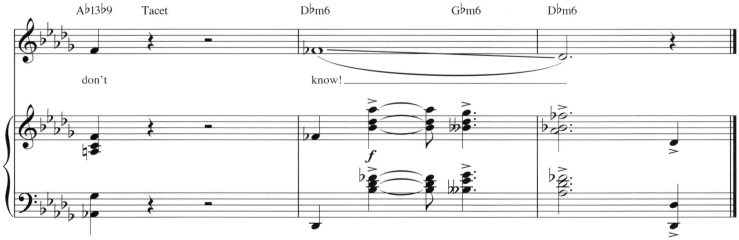

What Do I Need with Love

Lyrics by Dick Scanlan

Music by Jeanine Tesori

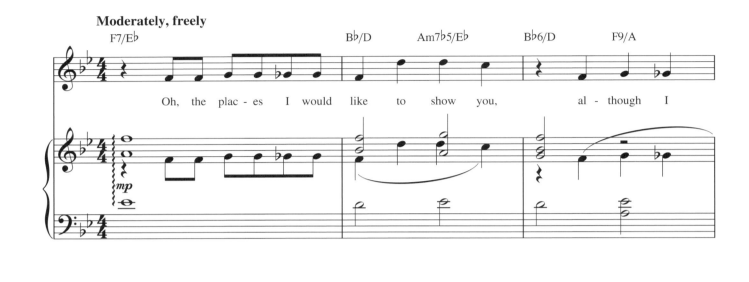

Copyright © 2001 That's Music To My Ears Ltd. and Thoroughly Modern Music Publishing Co.
International Copyright Secured   All Rights Reserved

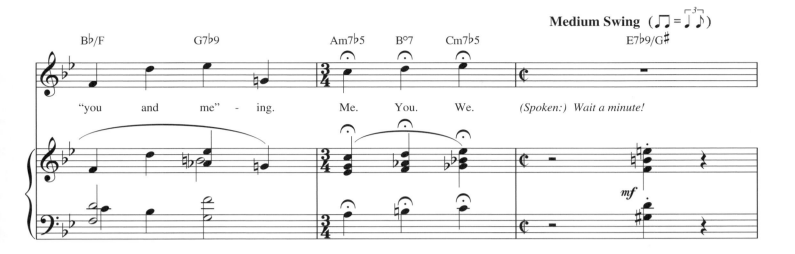

"you   and   me" - ing.   Me.   You.   We.   *(Spoken:) Wait a minute!*

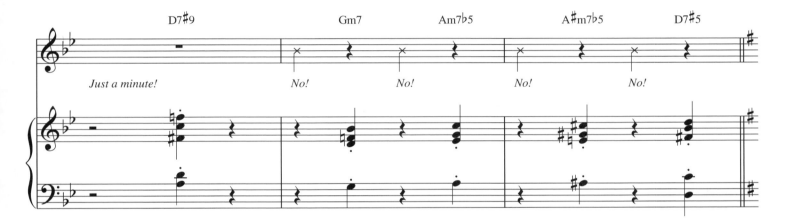

Just a minute!   *No!*   *No!*   *No!*   *No!*

I'm   a   Joe   with   just   one   aim: __   ev - 'ry   night   to   date   a
Al - ways   prac - tice   what   I   preach: __   keep   temp - ta - tion   out   of

dif - f'rent   dame. __   Call   each   one   of   'em   the   same   pet   name: __   "Hey,
eas - y   reach. __   Stick   to   dolls   who   wash   their   hair   in   bleach. __   I'm

54

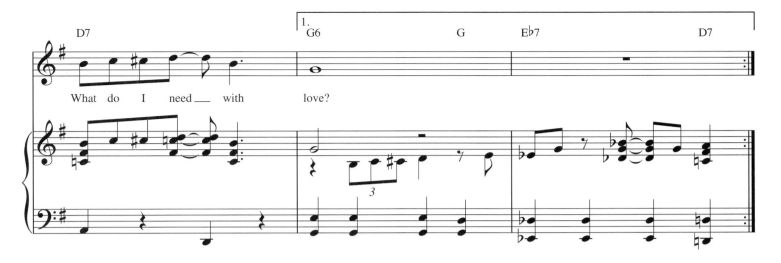

What do I need___ with love?

love?___ That was a near miss.

Talk a-bout a close shave.___ Flirt-ed with dis - as - ter.

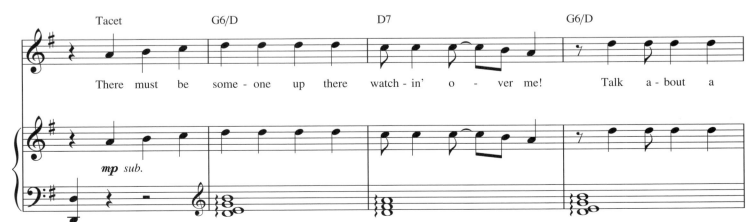

There must be some-one up there watch-in' o - ver me! Talk a-bout a

four - leaf clo - ver me. Pe - ter Rab - bit's miss - ing foot - sie

means I roll with - out a toot - sie. Got it good.___

What do I need___ with love?___ I

got it good.___ What do I need___ with love?___

Double time feel (no swing)

56

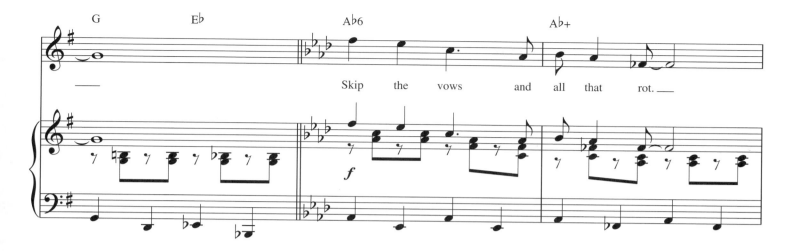

Skip the vows and all that rot. ___

Tell the min - is - ter that "I ___ do" ___ not.

Bright and breez - y is the, birds and bees - y is the,

free and eas - y is the life I got with - out

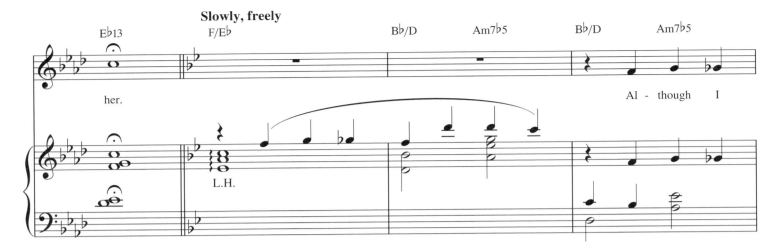

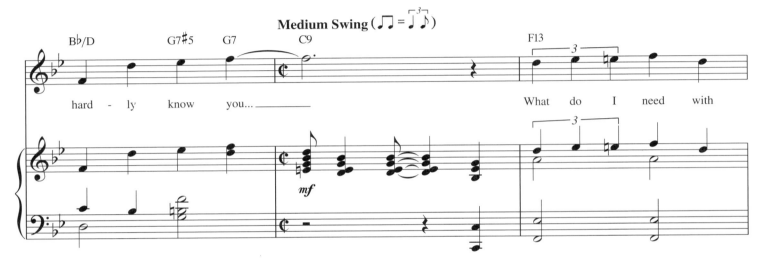

But now I

got _____ it _____

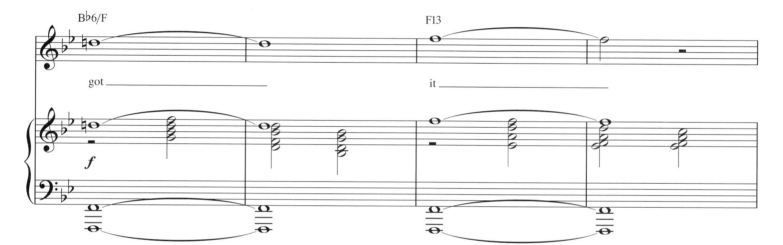

bad! _____

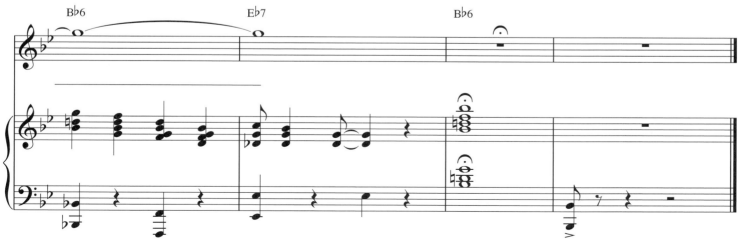

Only in New York

Lyrics by Dick Scanlan

Music by Jeanine Tesori

Copyright © 2001 That's Music To My Ears Ltd. and Thoroughly Modern Music Publishing Co.
International Copyright Secured   All Rights Reserved

Step right up ___ to Treas-ure Isle, ___ ev-'ry inch of it a sky-high mile. Fair-y-tale land. ___ On-ly in New York.

Hey, cas-tle build-er, ___ want the moon and noth-in' less? ___

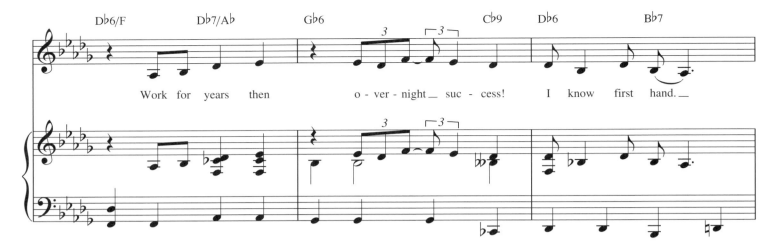

Work for years then o-ver-night__ suc-cess! I know first hand.__

On-ly in New York. Each day it's free ad-mis-sion to

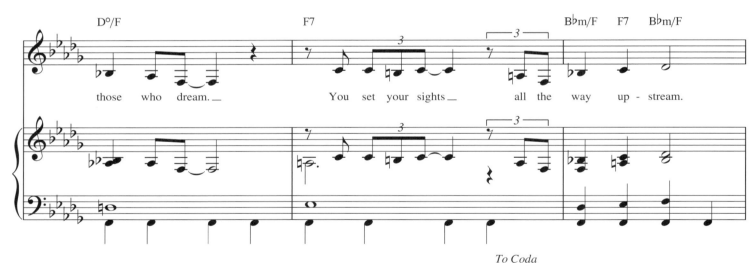

those who dream.__ You set your sights__ all the way up-stream.

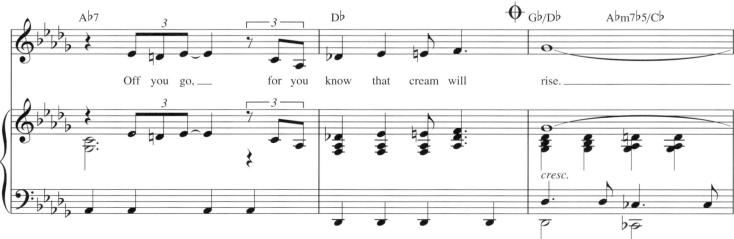

Off you go,__ for you know that cream will rise.__

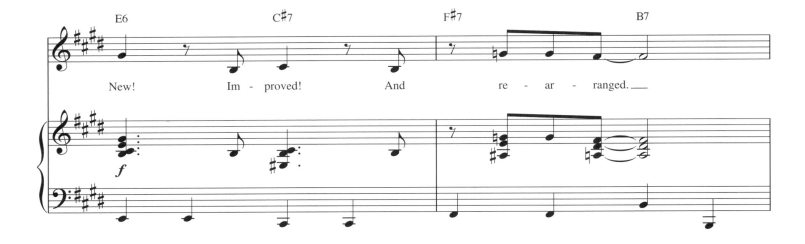

New! Im - proved! And re - ar - ranged.___

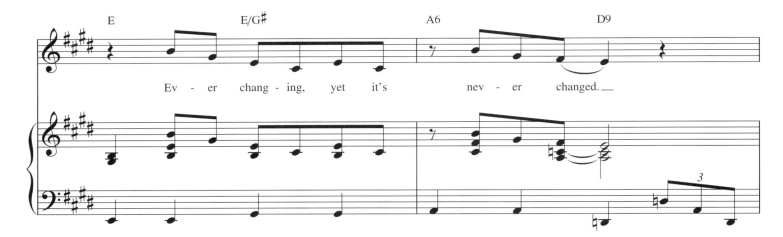

Ev - er chang - ing, yet it's nev - er changed.___

Life on com - mand!___ Hear what I'm say - ing!

Oh, but it's grand!___ That's why I'm stay - ing

right here, as planned. ____ On - ly in New York. ____

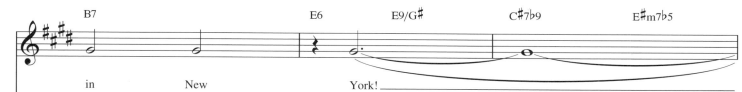

On - ly in New York. ____ On - ly ____

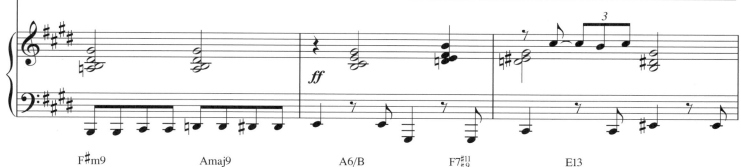

in New York! ____

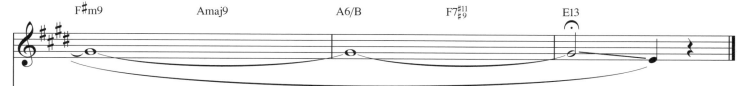

Jimmy

Additional Lyrics by Dick Scanlan

Original Music and Lyrics by Jay Thompson
Additional Music by Jeanine Tesori

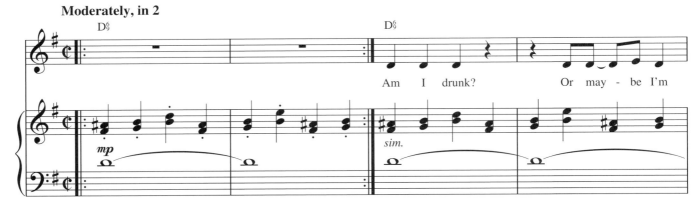

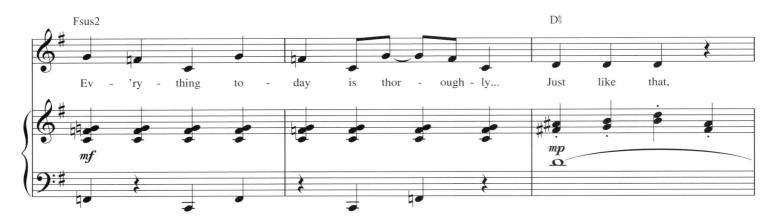

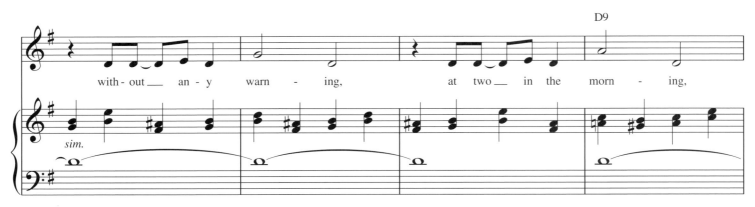

Original Music and Lyrics Copyright © 1967 Universal-Northern Music Co., Inc.
Additional Music and Lyrics Copyright © 2001 That's Music To My Ears Ltd. and Thoroughly Modern Music Publishing Co.
International Copyright Secured   All Rights Reserved

A♭7　　G♭sus2/B♭　　Bm6　　A♭7/C

he sud - den - ly... Ev - 'ry - thing to - day is thor - ough - ly...

mf

G6

Were there signs and I ___ did - n't see them? A ran - dom re -

mp　　*sim.*

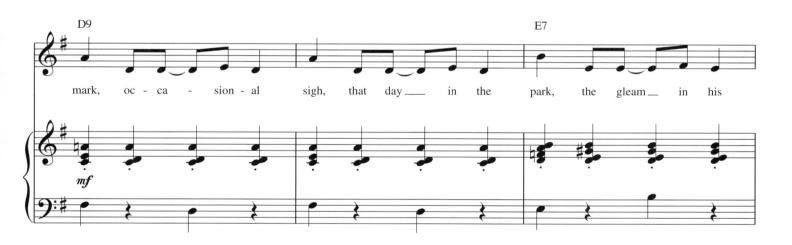

D9　　　　　　　　　　　E7

mark, oc - ca - sion - al sigh, that day ___ in the park, the gleam ___ in his

mf

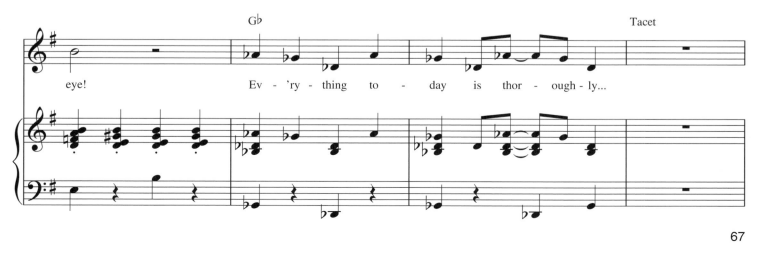

G♭　　　　　　　　　　Tacet

eye! Ev - 'ry - thing to - day is thor - ough - ly...

Ev - 'ry - thing to - day is thor - ough - ly...   Jim - my, oh,

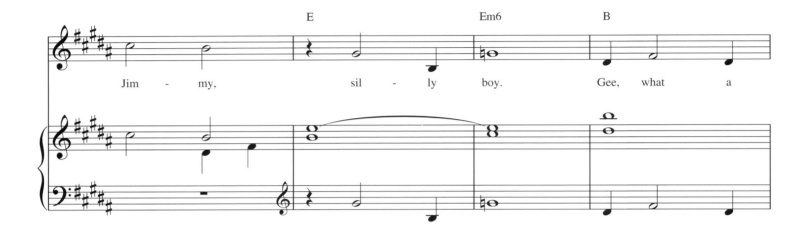

Jim - my,   sil - ly boy.   Gee, what a

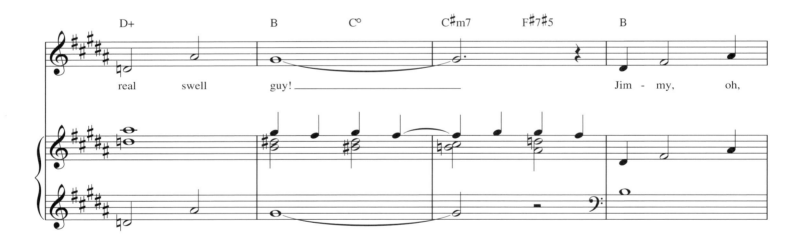

real swell guy! _____   Jim - my, oh,

Jim - my,   oh, what joy.   He makes my

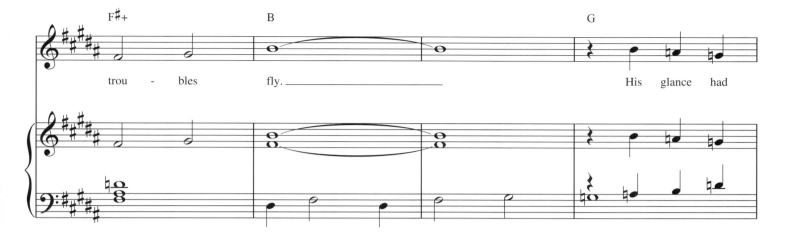

trou - bles fly. _____ His glance had

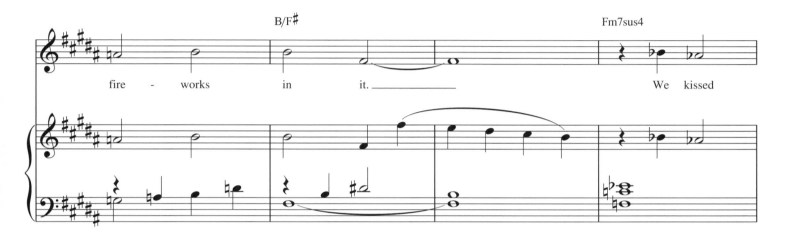

fire - works in it. _____ We kissed

my heart did a whiz - bang flip - flop, heav - en for a min - ute.

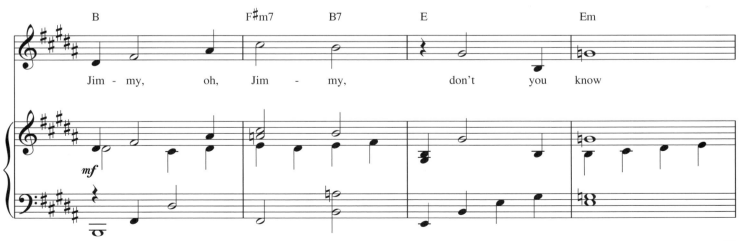

Jim - my, oh, Jim - my, don't you know

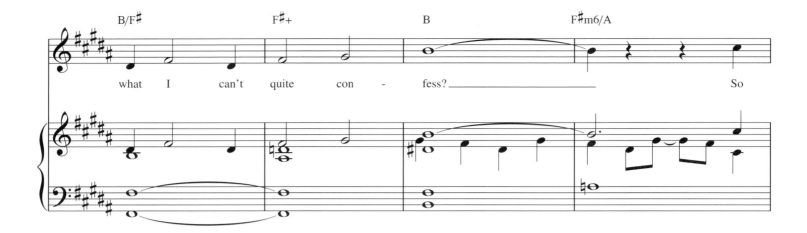

what I can't quite con - fess? _____ So

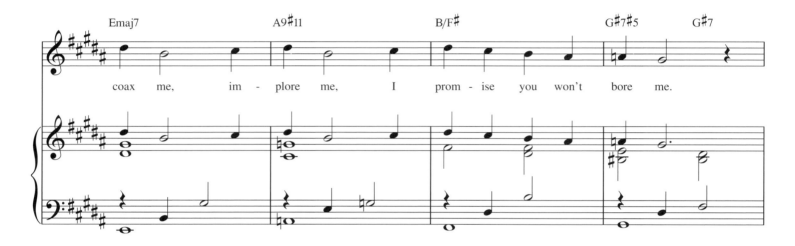

coax me, im - plore me, I prom - ise you won't bore me.

Jim - my, I might say yes. _____

Moderately, in 2

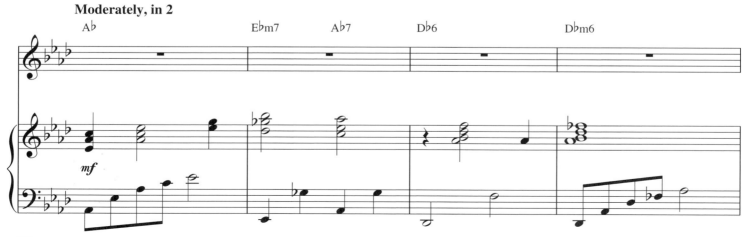

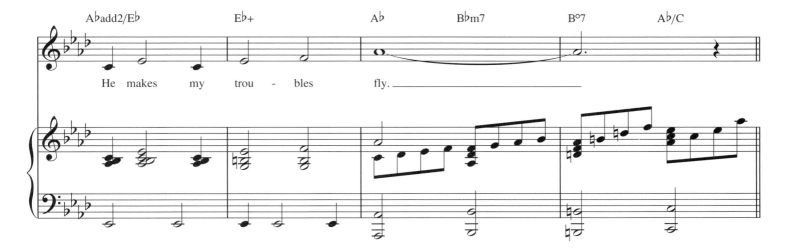

He makes my trou - bles fly. _____

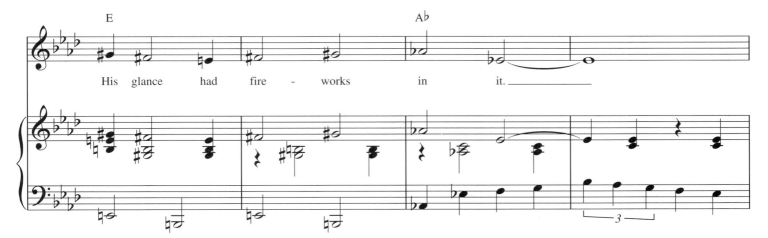

His glance had fire - works in it. _____

We kissed, my heart did a whiz - bang flip - flop,

Moderately, in 2

heav - en for a min - ute. So Jim - my, oh, Jim - my,

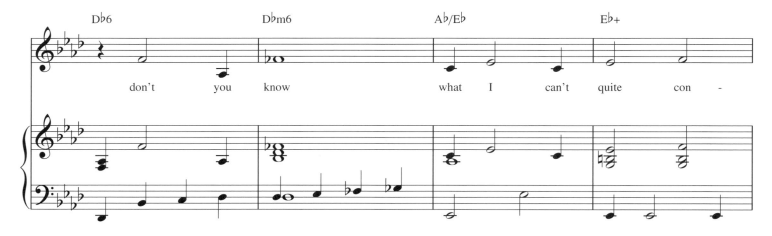

don't you know what I can't quite con-

Freely

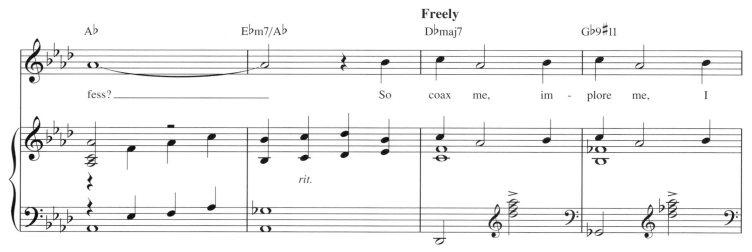

fess?_____ So coax me, im - plore me, I

prom - ise you won't bore me. Oh, Jim - my, I might say

yes._____

Forget About the Boy

Lyrics by Dick Scanlan

Music by Jeanine Tesori

Copyright © 2001 That's Music To My Ears Ltd. and Thoroughly Modern Music Publishing Co.
International Copyright Secured   All Rights Reserved

cross - er. For - get a - bout the boy. Pull the plug.
hal - le - luh!

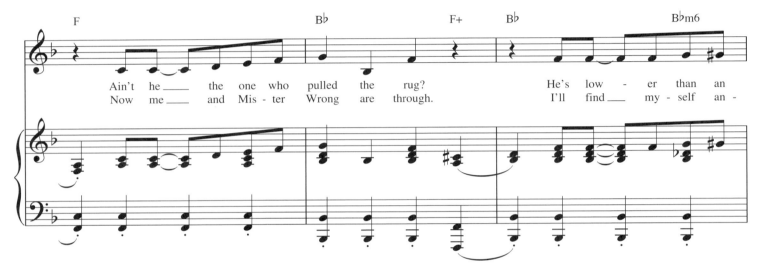

Ain't he ___ the one who pulled the rug? He's low - er than an
Now me ___ and Mis - ter Wrong are through. I'll find ___ my - self an -

al - ley cat, dirt - y ___ rat, and I flat -
oth - er beau who I ___ know is no rov -

ter.
er. } For - get a - bout ___ the boy.

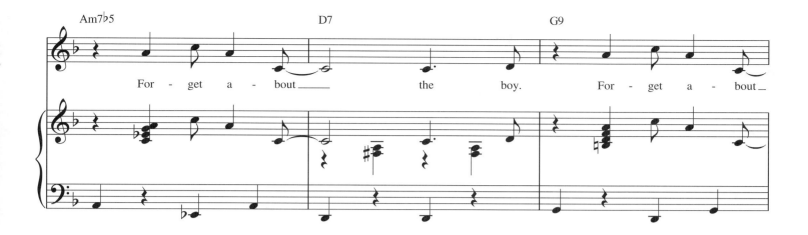

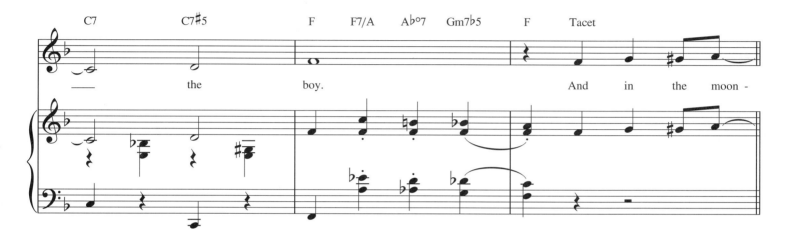

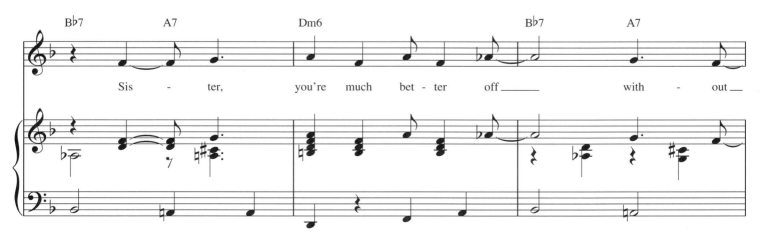

him. You can blow the blues a kiss good - bye, ___

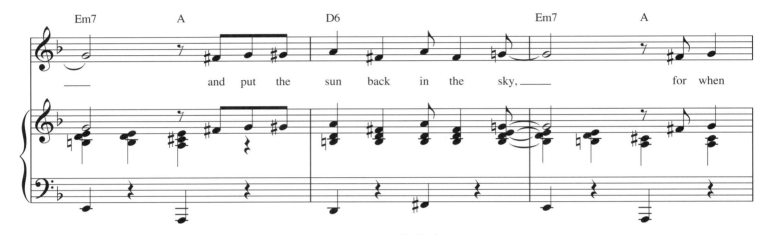

___ and put the sun back in the sky, ___ for when

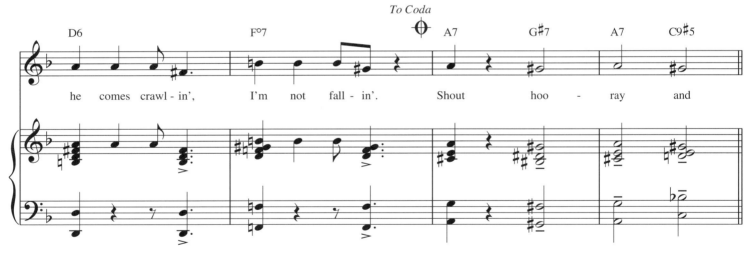

he comes crawl - in', I'm not fall - in'. Shout hoo - ray and

hal - le - luh! Now me ___ and Mis - ter Wrong are through.

I'll find ___ my-self an-oth-er beau who I ___ know is no

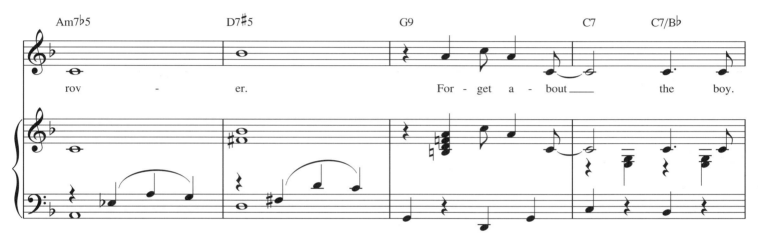

rov ___ er. For-get a-bout ___ the boy.

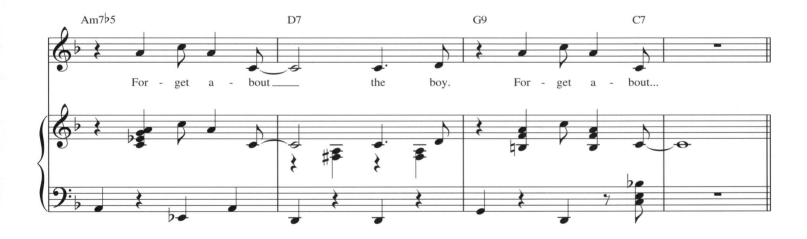

For-get a-bout ___ the boy. For-get a-bout...

Jim-my, ___ oh, Jim-my, Hor-ace, Dan-ny,

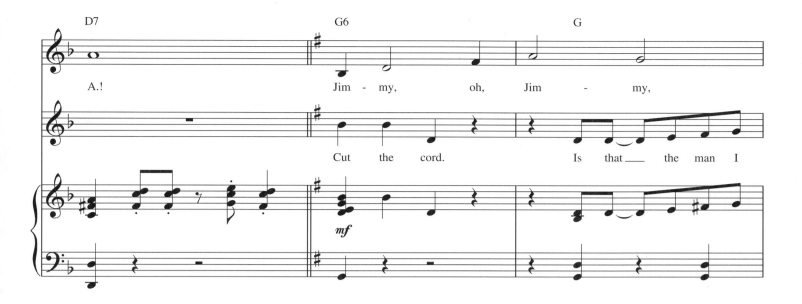

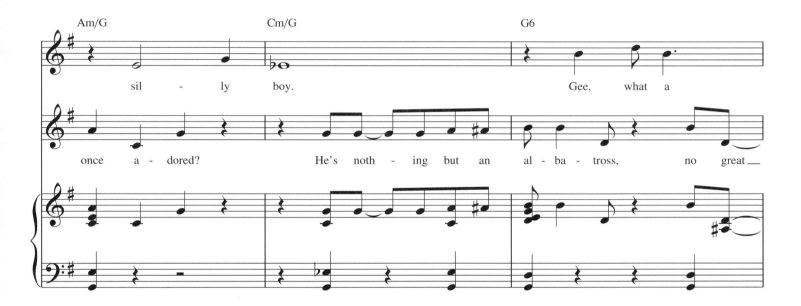

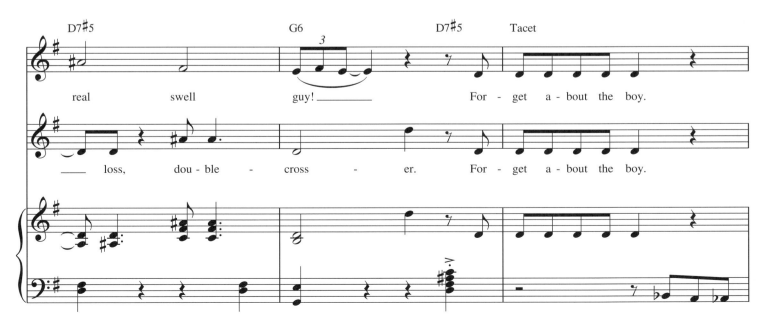

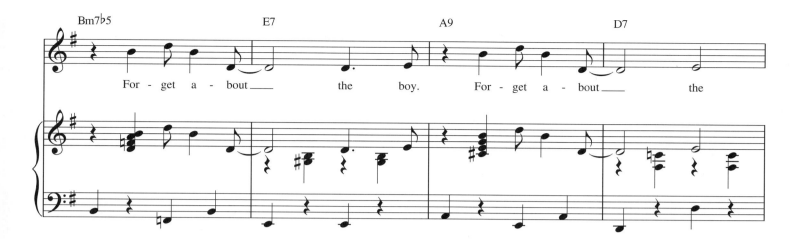

For - get a - bout ___ the boy. For - get a - bout ___ the

boy! ___

D.S. al Coda

Shout hoo - ray and

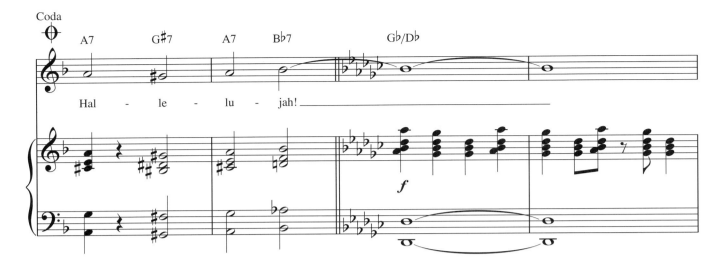

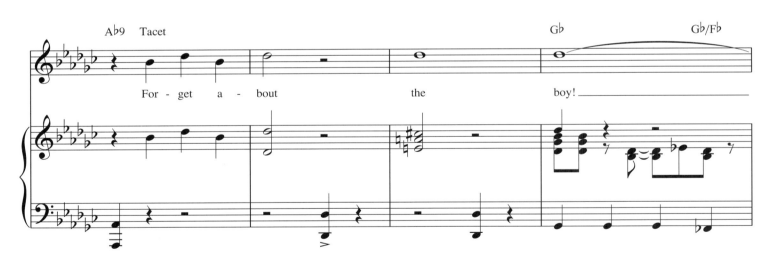

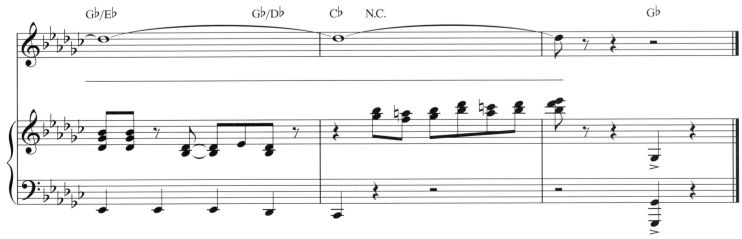

Ah! Sweet Mystery of Life/
I'm Falling in Love with Someone

Lyrics by Rida Johnson Young

Music by Victor Herbert

Grandly, romantically

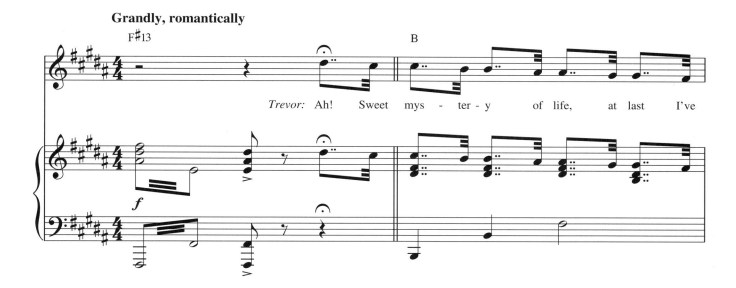

Trevor: Ah! Sweet mys - ter - y of life, at last I've

found thee. Ah! I know at last the se - cret of it

all. *Dorothy:* All the long - ing, seek - ing, striv - ing, wait - ing,

Ah! Sweet Mystery of Life
This Arrangement Copyright © 2003 Cherry Lane Music Company
International Copyright Secured   All Rights Reserved

I'm Falling in Love with Someone
This Arrangement Copyright © 2001 That's Music To My Ears Ltd.
International Copyright Secured   All Rights Reserved

yearn - ing,   the burn - ing   hopes, the   joy   and   i - dle   tears that

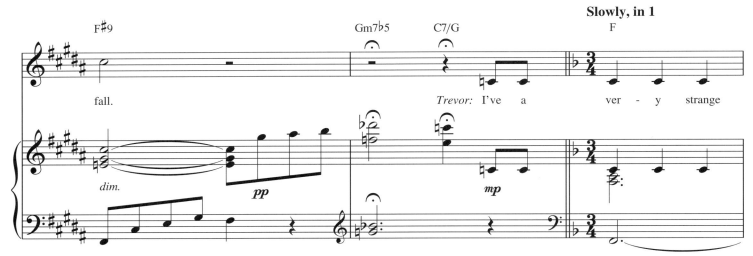

fall.   *Trevor:* I've a   ver - y   strange

Slowly, in 1

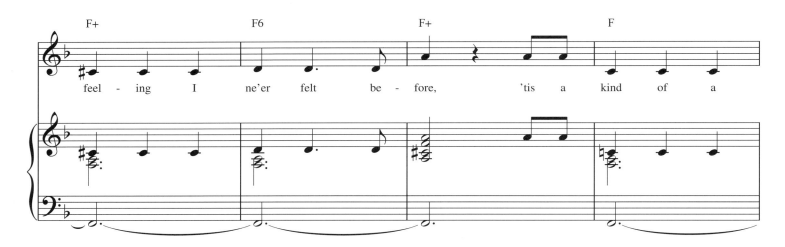

feel - ing I   ne'er felt be - fore,   'tis a   kind   of a

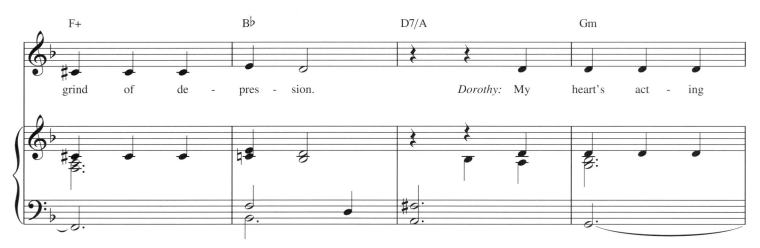

grind   of   de - pres - sion.   *Dorothy:* My   heart's   act - ing

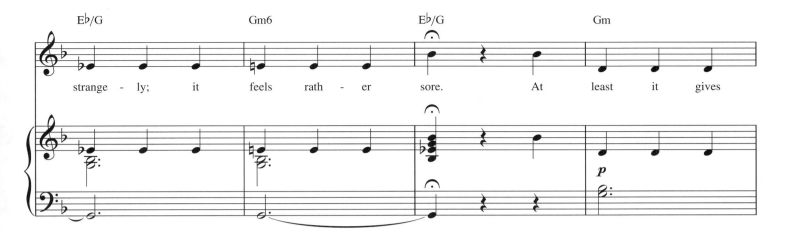

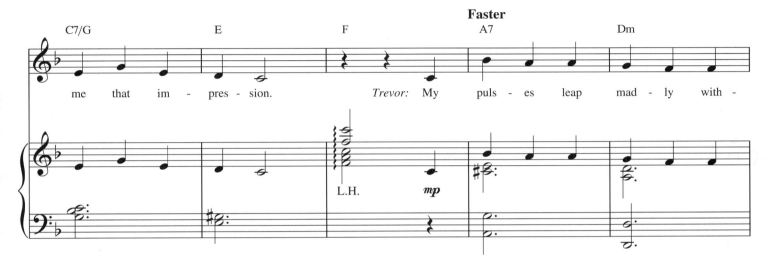

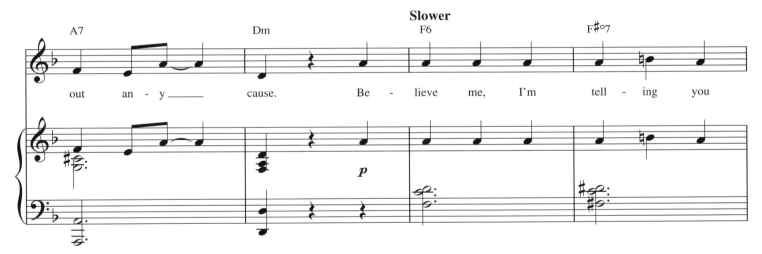

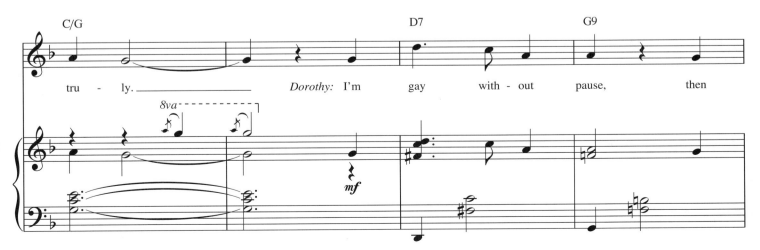

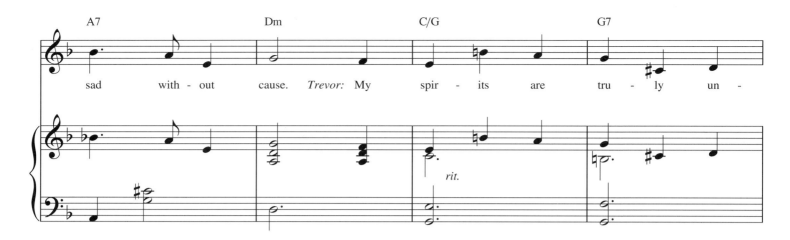

sad with - out cause. *Trevor:* My spir - its are tru - ly un -

ru - ly._____ For I'm fall - ing in love with

Waltz tempo

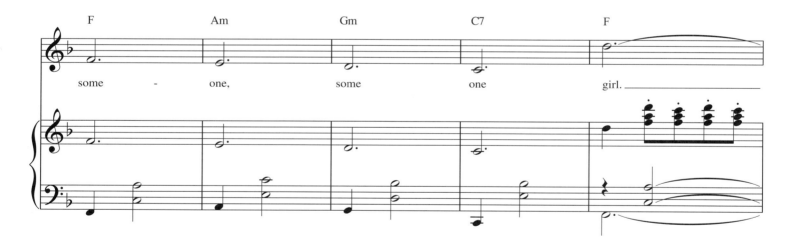

some - one, some one girl._____

_____ I'm fall - ing in love with some - one,

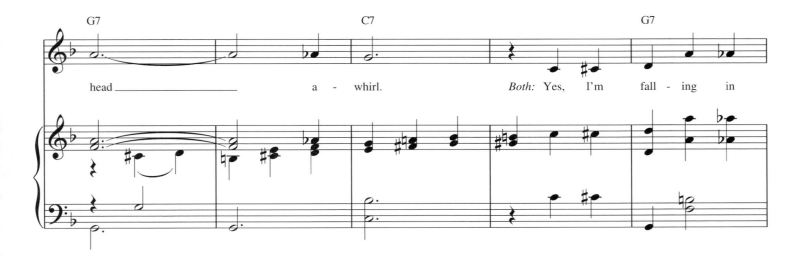

head _____ a - whirl. *Both:* Yes, I'm fall - ing in

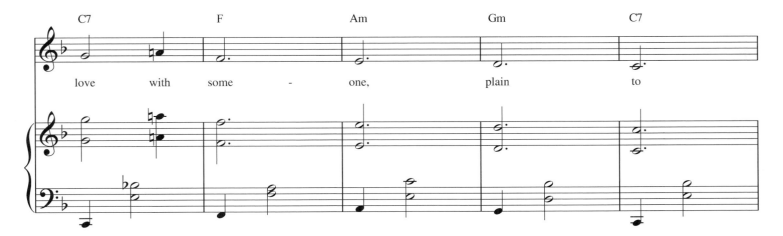

love with some - one, plain to

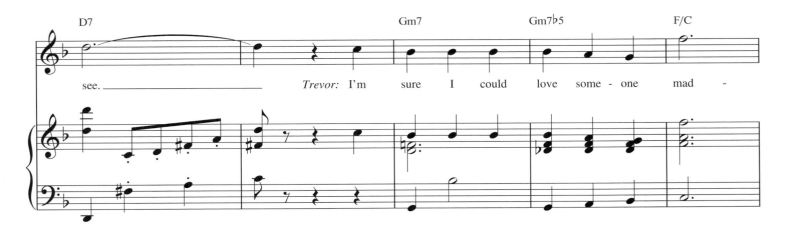

see. _____ *Trevor:* I'm sure I could love some - one mad -

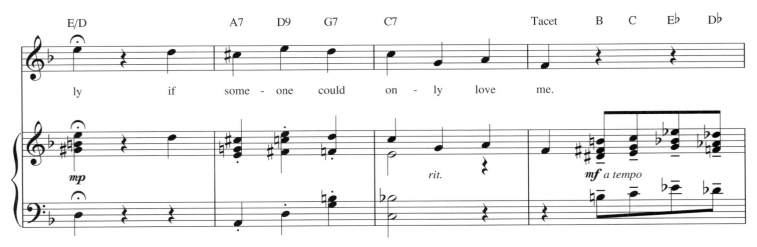

ly if some - one could on - ly love me.

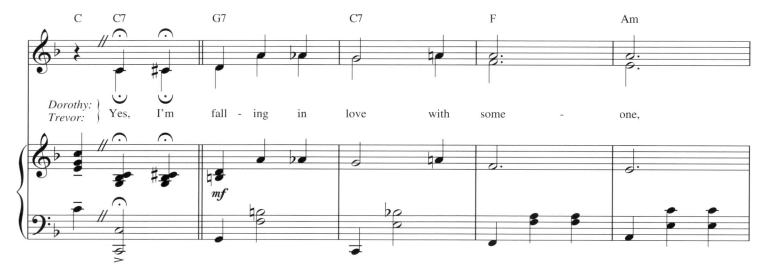

Dorothy: ⎫
Trevor: ⎬ Yes, I'm fall - ing in love with some - one,

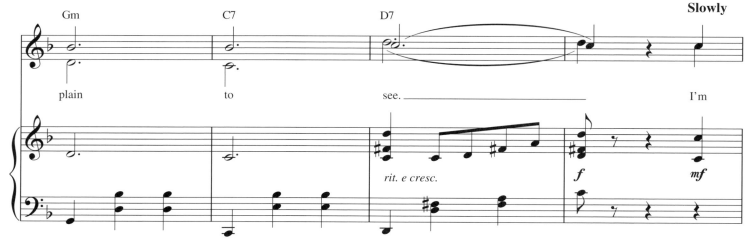

plain to see. _____ I'm

sure I could love some - one mad - ly if

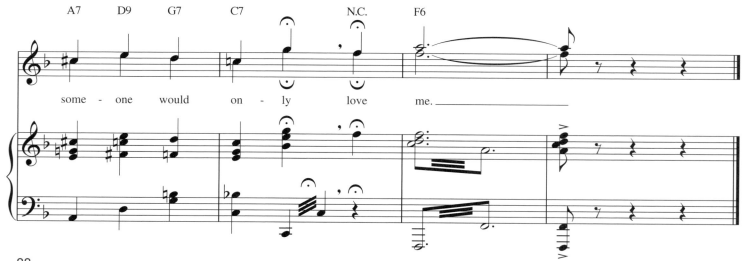

some - one would on - ly love me. _____

I Turned the Corner

Lyrics by Dick Scanlan

Music by Jeanine Tesori

Copyright © 2001 That's Music To My Ears Ltd. and Thoroughly Modern Music Publishing Co.
International Copyright Secured   All Rights Reserved

nues and parks. On their marks, rac - ing fast; quite a cast.

Mil - lions of peo - ple, pick an - y two: they could be just like

you and me used to be way back when, stran - gers, then

Slowly and freely (in 2)

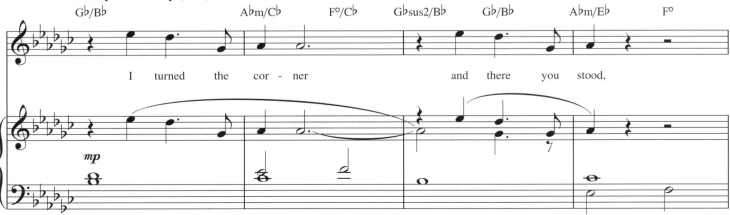

I turned the cor - ner and there you stood,

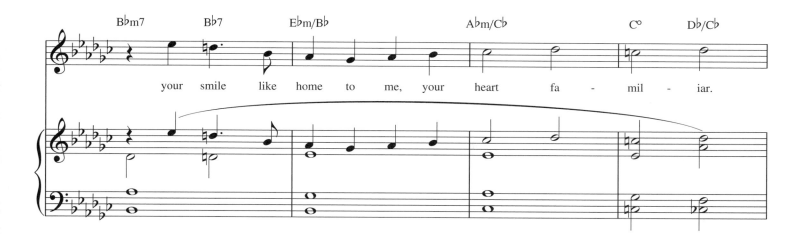

your smile like home to me, your heart fa - mil - iar.

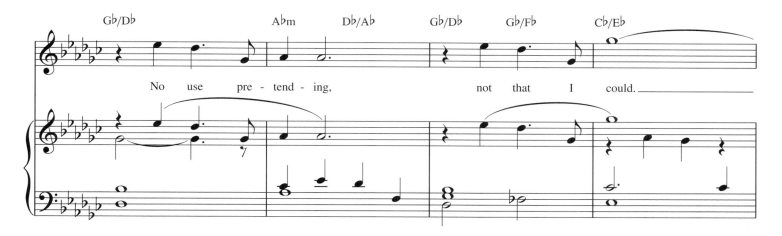

No use pre - tend - ing, not that I could. _____

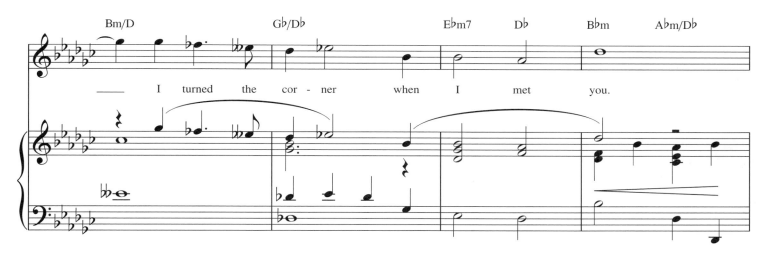

_____ I turned the cor - ner when I met you.

Moderately slow (in 2)

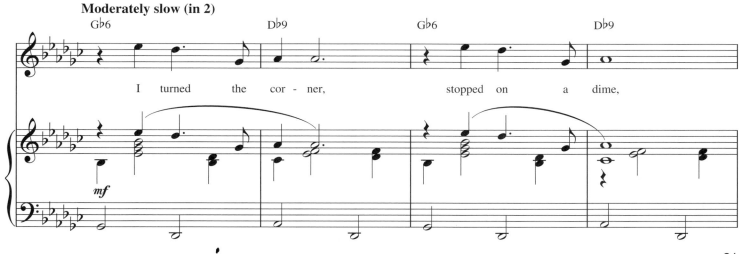

I turned the cor - ner, stopped on a dime,

like I re-mem-bered some-one long for-got-ten.

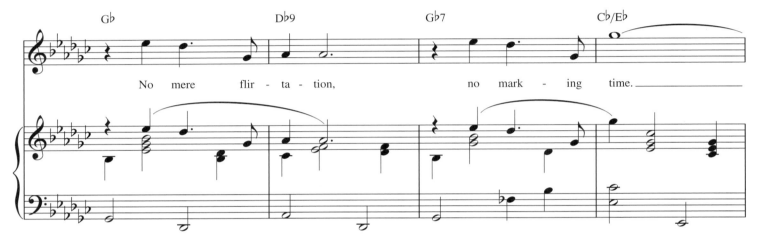

No mere flir-ta-tion, no mark-ing time.

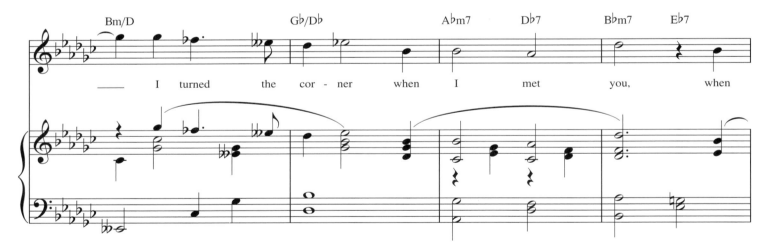

I turned the cor-ner when I met you, when

I met you. Was our en-coun-ter planned,

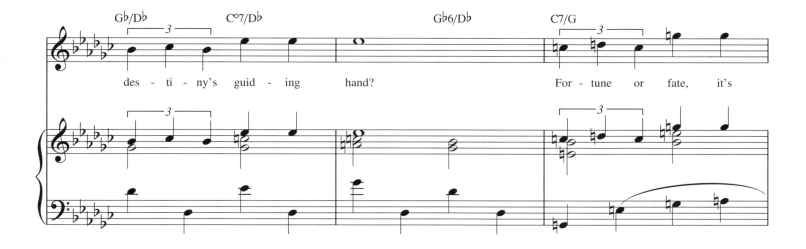

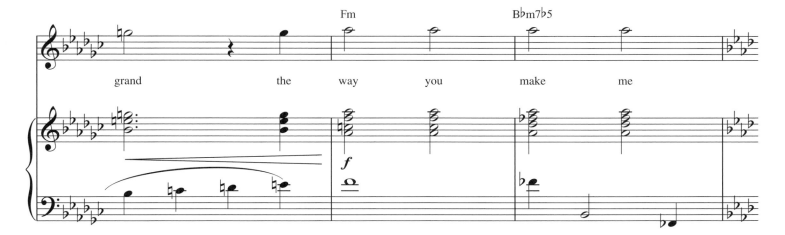

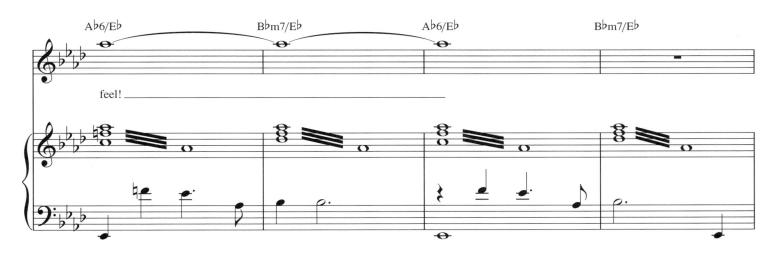

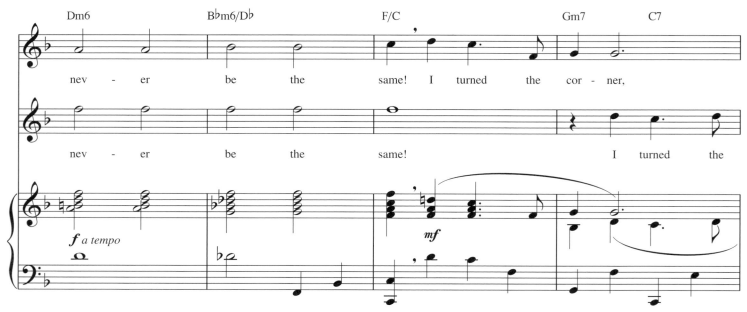

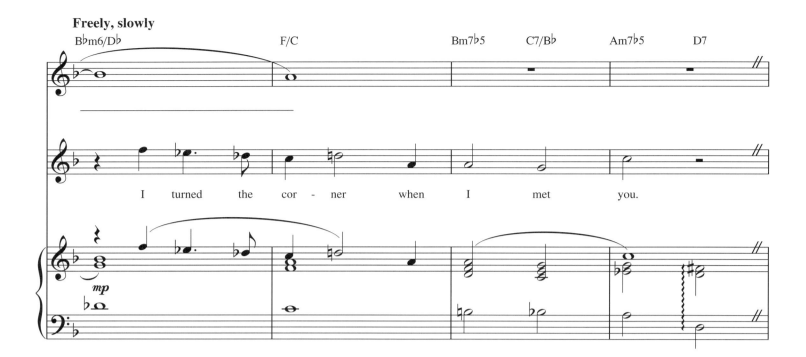

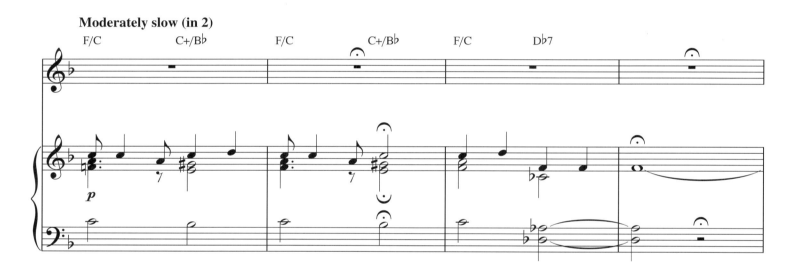

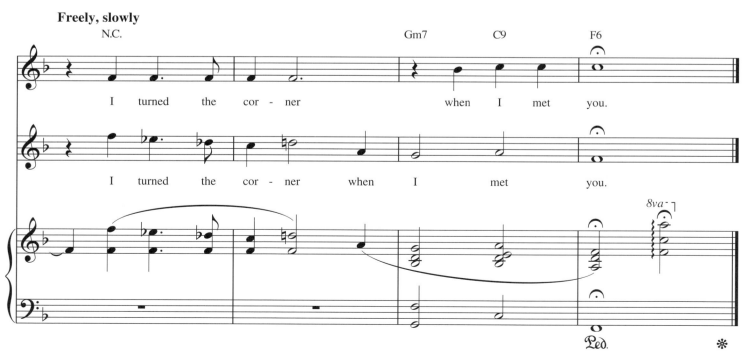

Long As I'm Here with You

Lyrics by Dick Scanlan

Music by Jeanine Tesori

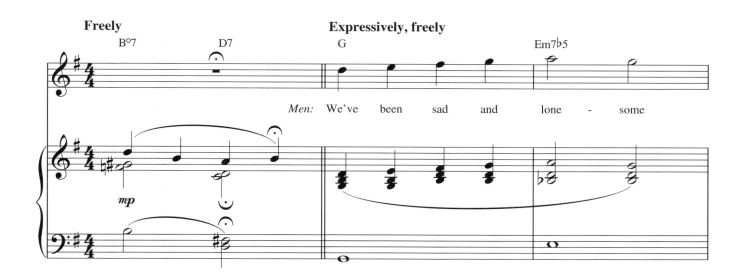

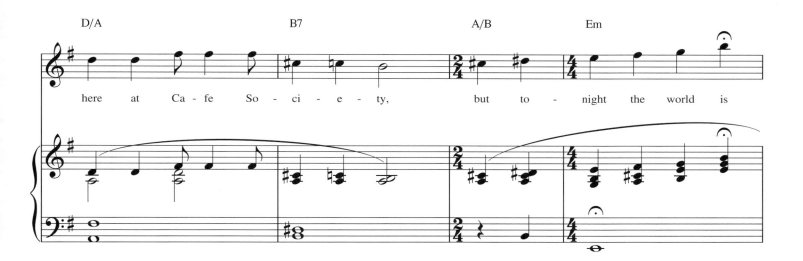

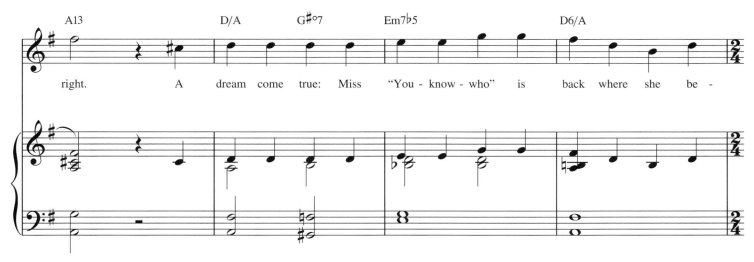

Copyright © 2001 That's Music To My Ears Ltd. and Thoroughly Modern Music Publishing Co.
International Copyright Secured   All Rights Reserved

Bright 2 ($\sqcap$ = $\sqcap^3$ ♩♪)

longs.   Ba da da da da ba da   da da da da_   ba

rot dat da da   ba da da da da   ba da da da_   da

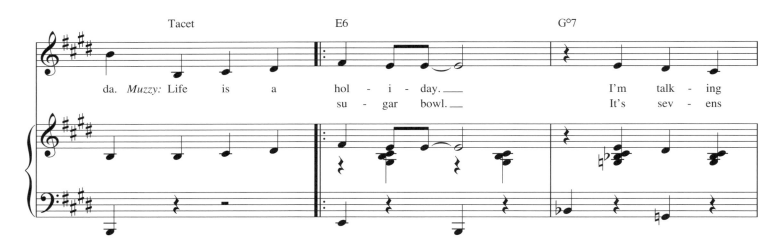

da. *Muzzy:* Life is a hol - i - day. _   I'm talk - ing
su - gar bowl. _   It's sev - ens

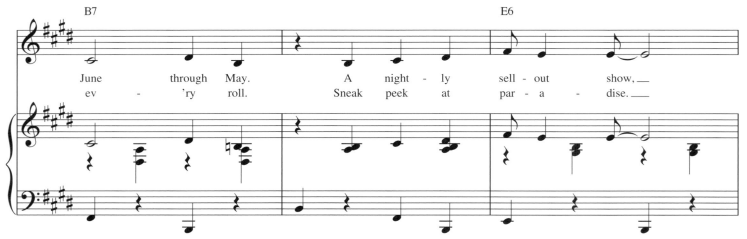

June   through May.   A night - ly sell - out show, _
ev - 'ry roll.   Sneak peek at par - a - dise. _

98

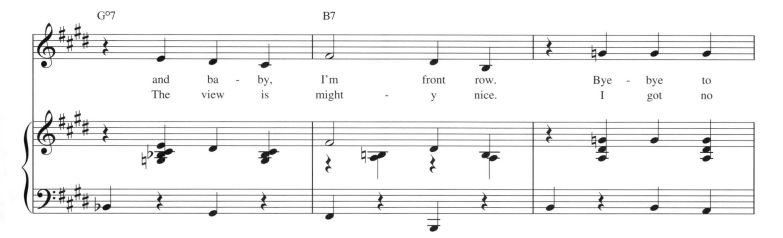

and ba - by, I'm front row. Bye - bye to
The view is might - y nice. I got no

lone - ly nights___ on - ly nights when the two of us___ can coo.___
blues to sing,___ choose to sing a mel - o - dy___ for two.___

Skies are sun - ny and___ clear, long as I'm here___
Hap - py end - ing is___ near, long as I'm here___

___ with you.

The world's a ___ with you. *Men:* Life is a hol - i - day. ___ I'm talk - ing June through May. A night - ly sell - out show, ___ and ba - by, I'm front row. *Muzzy:* I got no

blues to sing, __ choose to sing a mel - o - dy __ for two. __

__ Hap - py end - ing is __ near, long as I'm here __ with you.

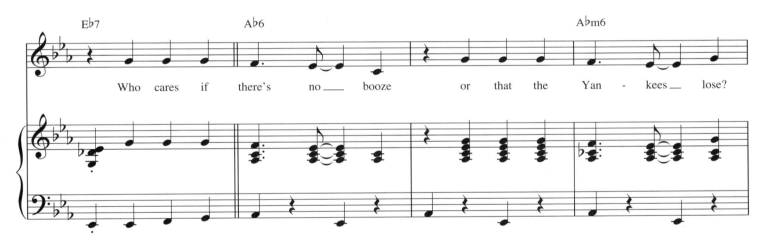

Who cares if there's no __ booze or that the Yan - kees __ lose?

Can't pay my in - come __ tax, but in spite of the facts,

Tacet / E6 / G°7 / B7

no one could ask for more. ___ Kid in a can - dy store. ___

E6 / G°7 / B7

The jack - pot has been hit. ___ I'm liv - ing proof of ___ it.

G#7

And as for all that ___ passed, call that ___ past.

C#7 / F#7 / B7

I found a heart that's true. What a red let - ter year long as I'm here ___

with you, and you, and you and you and

you and you and, yeah, you too. So hap-py, dear, ___

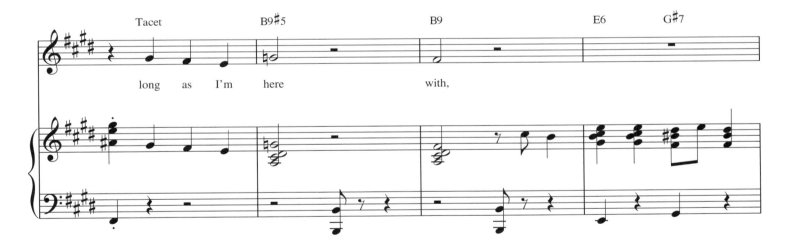

long as I'm here with,

long as I'm here ___ with you.

Gimme Gimme

Lyrics by Dick Scanlan

Music by Jeanine Tesori

Copyright © 2001 That's Music To My Ears Ltd. and Thoroughly Modern Music Publishing Co.
International Copyright Secured   All Rights Reserved

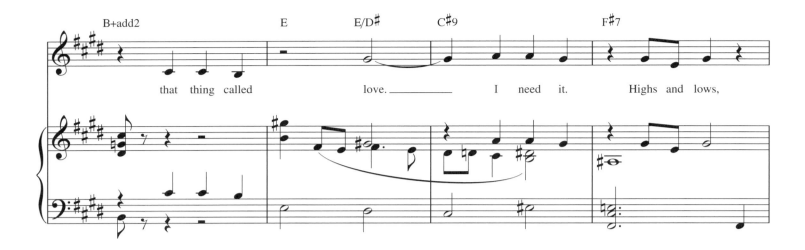

that thing called love. _____ I need it. Highs and lows,

tears and laugh-ter. Gim-me hap-py ev-er af-ter.

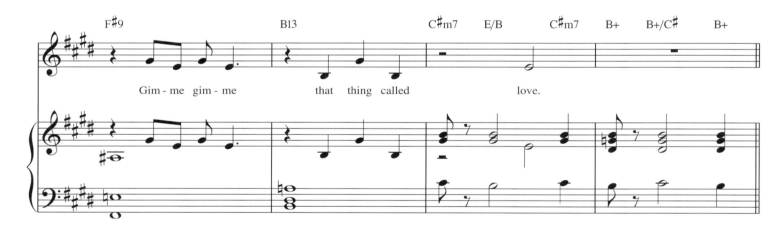

Gim-me gim-me that thing called love.

Moderately, with more confidence

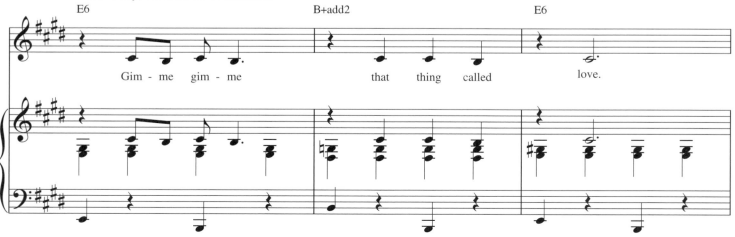

Gim-me gim-me that thing called love.

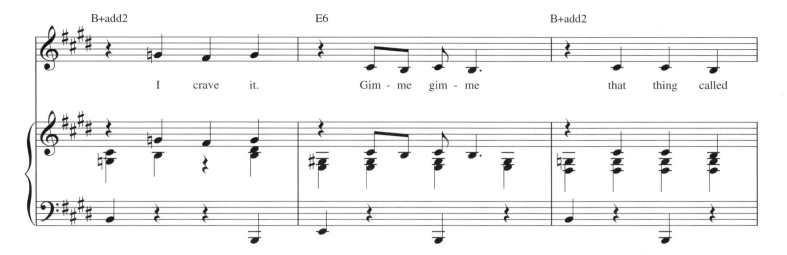

I crave it. Gim-me gim-me that thing called

love. I'll brave __ it. Thick 'n' thin,

rich or poor time. Gim-me years and I'll want more __ time.

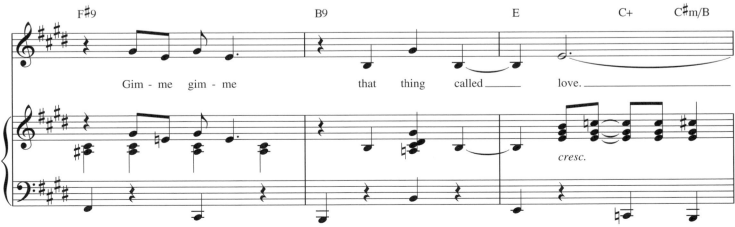

Gim-me gim-me that thing called __ love. __

Spirited, in 2

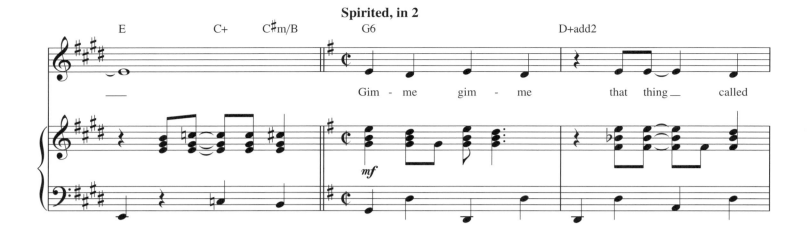

Gim - me gim - me that thing called ____ love. ____

Faster

I don't care ____ if he's a no - bod - y.

In my heart ____ he'll be a some - bod - y,

some - bod - y to love me. ____

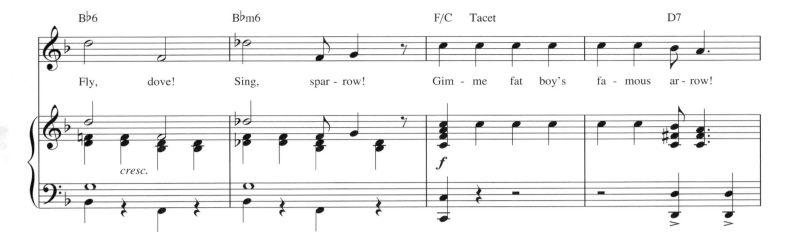

Fly, dove! Sing, spar-row! Gim - me fat boy's fa - mous ar-row!

Gim - me gim - me that thing called

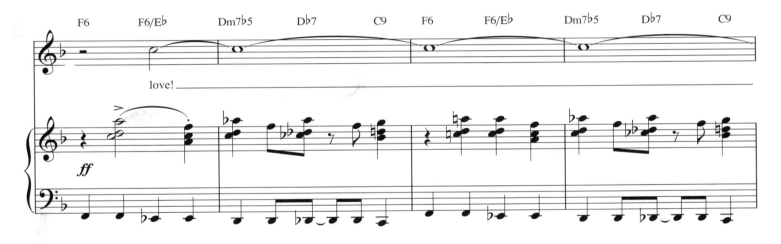

love!

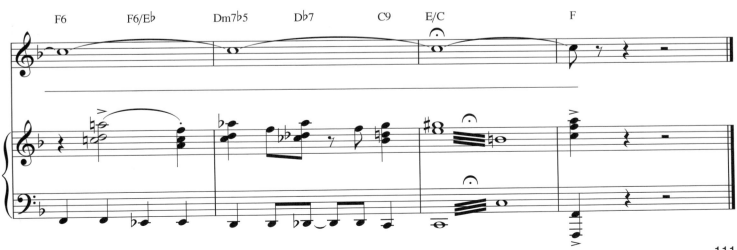

More Great Piano/Vocal Books from Cherry Lane

For a complete listing of Cherry Lane titles available, including contents listings, please visit our web site at

www.cherrylane.com

02500343	Almost Famous	$14.95
02501801	Amistad	$14.95
02502171	The Best of Boston	$17.95
02500144	Mary Chapin Carpenter – Party Doll and Other Favorites	$16.95
02502163	Mary Chapin Carpenter – Stones in the Road	$17.95
02502165	John Denver Anthology – Revised	$22.95
02502227	John Denver – A Celebration of Life	$14.95
02500002	John Denver Christmas	$14.95
02502166	John Denver's Greatest Hits	$17.95
02502151	John Denver – A Legacy in Song (Softcover)	$24.95
02502152	John Denver – A Legacy in Song (Hardcover)	$34.95
02500326	John Denver – The Wildlife Concert	$17.95
02509922	The Songs of Bob Dylan	$29.95
02500396	Linda Eder – Christmas Stays the Same	$17.95
02500175	Linda Eder – It's No Secret Anymore	$14.95
02502209	Linda Eder – It's Time	$17.95
02509912	Erroll Garner Songbook, Vol. 1	$17.95
02500270	Gilbert & Sullivan for Easy Piano	$12.95
02500318	Gladiator	$12.95
02502273	Gold & Glory: The Road to El Dorado	$16.95
02502126	Best of Guns N' Roses	$17.95
02502072	Guns N' Roses – Selections from Use Your Illusion I and II	$17.95
02500014	Sir Roland Hanna Collection	$19.95
02500352	Hanson – This Time Around	$16.95
02502134	Best of Lenny Kravitz	$12.95
02500012	Lenny Kravitz – 5	$16.95
02500381	Lenny Kravitz – Greatest Hits	$14.95
02500003	Dave Matthews Band – Before These Crowded Streets	$17.95
02502199	Dave Matthews Band – Crash	$17.95
02502192	Dave Matthews Band – Under the Table and Dreaming	$17.95
02500081	Natalie Merchant – Ophelia	$14.95
02500423	Natalie Merchant – Tigerlily	$14.95
02502204	The Best of Metallica	$17.95
02500407	O-Town	$14.95
02500010	Tom Paxton – The Honor of Your Company	$17.95
02507962	Peter, Paul & Mary – Holiday Concert	$17.95
02500145	Pokemon 2.B.A. Master	$12.95
02500026	The Prince of Egypt	$16.95
02502189	The Bonnie Raitt Collection	$22.95

02502230	Bonnie Raitt – Fundamental	$17.95
02502139	Bonnie Raitt – Longing in Their Hearts	$16.95
02502088	Bonnie Raitt – Luck of the Draw	$14.95
02507958	Bonnie Raitt – Nick of Time	$14.95
02502190	Bonnie Raitt – Road Tested	$24.95
02502218	Kenny Rogers – The Gift	$16.95
02500072	Saving Private Ryan	$14.95
02500197	SHeDAISY – The Whole SHeBANG	$14.95
02500414	SHREK	$14.95
02500166	Steely Dan – Anthology	$17.95
02500284	Steely Dan – Two Against Nature	$14.95
02500165	Best of Steely Dan	$14.95
02502132	Barbra Streisand – Back to Broadway	$19.95
02507969	Barbra Streisand – A Collection: Greatest Hits and More	$17.95
02502164	Barbra Streisand – The Concert	$22.95
02502228	Barbra Streisand – Higher Ground	$16.95
02500196	Barbra Streisand – A Love Like Ours	$16.95
02500280	Barbra Streisand – Timeless	$22.95
02503617	John Tesh – Avalon	$15.95
02502178	The John Tesh Collection	$17.95
02503623	John Tesh – A Family Christmas	$15.95
02505511	John Tesh – Favorites for Easy Piano	$12.95
02503630	John Tesh – Grand Passion	$16.95
02500124	John Tesh – One World	$14.95
02500307	John Tesh – Pure Movies 2	$16.95
02502175	Tower of Power – Silver Anniversary	$17.95
02502198	The "Weird Al" Yankovic Anthology	$17.95
02502217	Trisha Yearwood – A Collection of Hits	$16.95
02500334	Maury Yeston – December Songs	$17.95
02502225	The Maury Yeston Songbook	$19.95

See your local music dealer or contact:

CHERRY LANE
MUSIC COMPANY
6 East 32nd Street, New York, NY 10016

EXCLUSIVELY DISTRIBUTED BY
HAL•LEONARD®
CORPORATION
7777 W. BLUEMOUND RD. P.O. BOX 13819 MILWAUKEE, WI 53213

Prices, contents and availability subject to change without notice.